CROSS STITCH CATS

Richard Box

with Sue Fielding

B.T. Batsford Ltd, London

DEDICATION
For our furry, feline friends

ACKNOWLEDGEMENTS
This book has been compiled by a number of cross stitch embroiderers and cat lovers to whom I am eternally indebted and without whom the book would not have been possible. Sue Fielding, 'The Embroiderer in Chief', has not only stitched a number of the main projects and supplied the technical information, but has also supervised an entire team of enthusiasts who have devoted their energies and many months of their time embroidering all the other projects. I am extremely grateful to Teresa Ball, Jehanne Boulton, Joyce Brough, Bernice Brown, Gill Brown, Beryl Bowcott, Ruth Fitzgerald, Maria-Jose Gannon, Pauline Garnham, Marcia Gooder, Elizabeth Hadwick, Rob Halbert, Jennie Hubbard, Elizabeth Kelly, Jill Milne, Kitty Mogford, Dallas Percy, Liz Philips, Pat Ripley, Marion Roden, Joy Spencer, Jessie Street, Freda Taylor and June Thorn. I would also like to thank Celia Johnson for word-processing the final text, Michael Haworth for drawing the stitch diagrams and Dr Andrew Lund for producing the charts (using Easy-Cross De Luxe, supplied by Fulford Software Solutions).

My thanks to Coats Crafts, DMC Creative World and Madeira for supplying all the materials and threads, to Framecraft and Francesca Lawrence for accessories for the detailed projects, and to all those listed in the bibliography who have helped me with pictorial inspiration and research.

Finally, I am pleased to thank Venetia Penfold and Emma Clegg, my editors, for their help, kind reassurances and for commissioning this book for your pleasure.

First published in 1998 by
B.T. Batsford Ltd
583 Fulham Road
London SW6 5BY

A catalogue record for this book is available from the British Library.

ISBN 0 7134 8326 1

Printed in Hong Kong

Photography by Michael Wicks
Illustrations by Michael Haworth
Charts by Dr Andrew Lund
Designed by DWN Ltd, London

NOTE ON CHARTS USED IN THIS BOOK
Colours appearing on charts in this book are not necessarily accurate. Embroiderers should follow the thread number guides and follow the black-and-white charts. Charts appearing on two pages have extra lines of symbols to show overlap.

CONTENTS

INTRODUCTION

This book has been composed especially for cat lovers and cross stitch enthusiasts of all abilities. The projects featured here are star-rated according to their complexity, from one star to three, three being the most complex. The book combines one of the most popular of all embroidery stitches with one of the most favourite subjects. Both cross stitch and cats have a chequered history and were not always as popular as they are today, yet out of their history comes an overriding sense of respect and admiration for both the craft and the animal.

The precise origin of cross stitch has yet to be discovered, the earliest known piece probably dating back as far as AD 700, found in Egypt and believed to be Coptic. In England the first flowering of popularity blossomed during the sixteenth century when there appeared a great variety of stitched hangings, carpets and furniture coverings. These were embroidered by the grand ladies of the court, castles and manor houses, who used cross stitch (gros point) and half cross stitch (petit point) alongside other canvas work stitches. In the comfort of their own homes these amateurs were able to recreate with their needles the commercial loom-woven tapestry style. During this period of the English Renaissance, every lady and educated girl would embroider a 'sampler' as a record of stitch types and various patterns to which she may refer when needed. Stitches and patterns were either passed from one person to another or derived from pattern books. The first known is James Boler's *The Needle's Excellency*, thought to have been published originally in Germany in 1597, and which reached its twelfth edition in England in 1640.

Over the next few centuries, many scholars and historians state that cross stitch declined in popularity and was to be found mainly on samplers. They represents for us today a particular period of cross stitch history which appears to be confined to the teaching of moral lessons to little girls either at home or at Dame Schools. The many examples that exist have their own peculiar charm and are splendid examples of patience and skill. However, as Helen Rhodes writes in her book *Cross Stitch in 1959*, 'as far as teaching the elements of design or a love of embroidery was concerned they can be of no use at all'. Indeed, there is an instance, probably apocryphal, where a young girl must have been compelled to cross stitch her sampler under great duress as it bears the heartfelt legend 'This was worked by Mary Pitt who hated every stitch of it'.

In the early part of the nineteenth century came the invention of aniline dyes in Germany. Subsequent production of new brightly coloured wools then became available. Enterprising entrepreneurs produced numerous coloured charts with bouquets of large flowers and started a craze for 'Berlin wool work', a form of cross stitch in wool, to which many a gentlewoman and some gentlemen became addicted. In the 1920s a group of enthusiasts inspired by Louisa Pesel resurrected the earlier and finer type of cross stitch, together with more complex and traditional stitches. Classes were run, groups were formed and magazines were published, all of which generated an enormous interest which is still expanding today for men as well as women. This book is intended to perpetuate this interest for the cross stitch embroiderer and for the cat lover.

Indeed, cats are also a continual source of fascination. Of all domestic animals they are perhaps the only ones to live intimately with human beings at the same time as preserving their independence. The curiously sudden switch from tame pets to wild creatures and vice versa seems a contradiction but creates great interest in these creatures. They have also had a history of contradictory treatment.

Over three thousand years ago cats were bejewelled and worshipped in the temples of Pasht in ancient Egypt. The word 'puss' is believed to have derived from the name of this love goddess. They were even regarded as sacred. The punishment for killing a cat was death, and when they died the entire household went into deep mourning.

In the classical times of the first millenium BC, cats were beginning to spread around Europe and Asia. Artistic representations and skeletal remains from about 500 BC are often found at archaeological sites. Cats were probably valued as pest destroyers or even as fireside pets rather than as numinous beings. The Romans adopted cats for this reason. Hitherto, tame weasels were the standard pest controllers. However, it seems that the cats drove out the weasels, increased in numbers and became a desirable part of all respectable households in the Roman Empire.

Looking eastwards, it is believed that the Chinese knew the domestic cat before the Europeans had ever heard of it. In both China and Japan, cats were used to protect silkworms

from rodents. Cats in China were often called 'Tama', meaning jewel, because they were so highly valued for their services. Burmese, Siamese and Korats are all considered to be ancient breeds. Certainly they all appear in a collection of Thai manuscripts dating between circa AD 1350 and circa 1767, all acknowledging the high esteem with which Orientals regarded their cats. Long-haired cats from Iran (ancient Persia) and from Turkey are known to have been in existence for a long time before they were adopted by Europeans and were likewise highly regarded.

It is thought that the Romans brought the cat to England and for over a thousand years they were regarded as useful pets. The value of their usefulness was such that certain monetary laws were written about them. Yet from the late Middle Ages onwards, the feline population of Europe was to experience several centuries of torture, torment and termination. In 1484 Pope Innocent VIII officially declared war on them because it had recently been discovered that cats not only had once been involved in ancient rituals but also were still being worshipped in certain parts of Northern Europe. The minds of otherwise normal people were turned toward a frenzy of feline fatality. The ignorant and superstitious in authority from the Church downward proclaimed that cats were evil creatures, agents of the Devil and familiars of witches.

Fortunately, there are a number of recorded exceptions to this reign of feline prejudice. You will read in the main text of this book some extracts from the accounts of more enlightened persons who were all cat lovers and cherishing owners, such as Michel de Montaigne (1533–1592), Thomas Fuller (1668–1661) and George Louis Leclerc de Buffon (1707–1788). Added to these, Cardinal Richelieu (1585–1642) shared his home with fourteen cats to whom he bequeathed his entire fortune when he died, and even the

King of France himself, Louis XV, is said to have rebuked his courtiers severely for teasing his pet white Persian cat.

Indeed, happier days for cats were gradually reinstated. The eighteenth century's period of enlightenment had gradually swept away a good deal of ignorance and superstition. By the middle of the nineteenth century, people were becoming more humane and understanding about the process of evolution following the publication of Darwin's works. On 16th July, 1871, the artist and cat lover, Harrison Weir, organised the first ever cat show. Maybe Crystal Palace was not exactly one of the Temples of Pasht, but it was probably this single event which put the final seal of approval upon our furry friends, which continues to this very day. Long may it last!

Somewhere the Goddess smiles and everything
between Cat and Man is marvellous.
From *The Cat* (1979) by Anna Pollard

CHAPTER ONE

MATERIALS AND TECHNIQUES

This chapter lists and describes the various materials and equipment needed for cross stitch embroidery. It also explains the basic techniques and methods involved. Those of you who are just starting may find it helpful to refer to this chapter quite often as you proceed to embroider your first few projects.

MATERIALS

Fabrics and threads combine to make the form of cross stitch embroidery. It is important to select the threads carefully and then you can enjoy the whole working process.

FABRICS

The cross stitch projects in this book use the 'counted thread' technique. The 'thread count' refers to the number of threads per inch of fabric and calculating this means that you can transfer your understanding of the chart to the fabric. Fabrics vary considerably in the number of threads or 'counts' to the inch, depending on the relative density of the weave.

There are many types of fabric which can be used for cross stitch, but the projects in this book use just aida.

Aida

This is a firm, strong fabric, usually made of cotton. It is the most popular of all fabrics for cross stitching as it is easy to see the holes through which the needle passes. Aida can be purchased in a variety of colours and in various numbers of 'counts' to the inch.

Evenweave

Evenweave fabrics can be made of linen, cotton, synthetic fibres or a mixture of any of these. Evenweave fabric has the same number of threads per inch along both the warp and weft of the fabric. This ensures that the threads can easily be counted and that the crosses you stitch will be regular in

size and perfectly square. You can purchase them in a variety of colours and in various numbers of 'counts' to the inch. It is helpful to prevent the edges of the evenweave fabrics from fraying either by overcasting them with an overlocking machine, by hand, with a zig-zag stitch on a domestic sewing machine, or even by binding the edges with tape, bias binding or ribbon.

Canvas

This is a rigid fabric formed by single or double threads woven into an open-weave grid. It can be purchased in natural brown colours and white as well as in various numbers of counts to the inch. The edges need the same protection as all evenweave fabrics, not only to stop them from fraying but also to prevent the embroidery threads from catching and snagging.

Waste Canvas

When you become more experienced, you may like to use this fabric. It can be placed over any cloth which is unsuitable for cross stitch, such as felt, knitting and any irregularly woven material. After the cross stitch embroidery is completed, the canvas is dampened in order to loosen the glue which holds the threads together; each thread is then drawn out leaving just the embroidery on the cloth.

THREADS

Every day new and exciting threads appear on the market. They range from rough to smooth, thick to thin and

from matt to shiny and include a wonderful selection of metallic threads. All of them can be purchased in every imaginable colour.

Stranded Threads

Stranded cottons are the most commonly used for working counted cross stitch onto the background fabric of aida, evenweave and waste canvas. DMC, Anchor and Madeira all produce good quality stranded cottons in a vast array of splendid colours. Each thread has six strands which can be split to suit the count of the fabric to be embroidered. A number of other threads are also available which can be used on their own or integrated with cotton threads. Although these have not been used in the illustrated projects in this book, it is perfectly possible for you to include them to give variation in the textured surface in any of the projects you choose to embroider.

Sewing Thread

This is not only used to overcast the edges of your fabric but also to tack the outer edges and central line of your design (see page 15). It is advisable to use a similar colour and tone of thread to that of the fabric; you will need to see the thread, but when drawn out at the completion of the project it may leave slight traces of fibre which will not be too evident if they are the same colour as the fabric.

WOOL

There are three types of wool used in canvas work today: crewel wool, standard tapestry wool and stranded tapestry wool, as described below.

Crewel Wool

This is very fine and is most often used in crewel work of which the most recognisable form is Jacobean embroidery. However, crewel wool can also be used on a small scale on fine canvas to produce a miniature form of canvas embroidery.

Tapestry Wool

This comes in two forms, standard and stranded. The standard cannot be split. The stranded can be used as a tapestry wool or it can be split into three strands, each of which has the same strength and fineness as crewel wool and can be used as such.

Stranded cottons have been used for all the projects in this book. However, as long as you match the density, colour and tonal value of these threads you can replace them with others. Perlé cotton is a shiny twisted thread, flower threads are made from cotton with a matt surface and rayon threads, such as Anchor Marlitt, are very shiny. Even ribbons are various and versatile, ranging from matt to shiny and it is possible also to use beads to give glamour and richness to any of these projects.

ESSENTIAL EQUIPMENT

Tools and equipment are all-important items for the creation of cross stitch embroidery. They need to be of good quality materials and to be securely made in order to make the process of using it for embroidery safe as well as pleasurable.

Scissors

Every work box should have three pairs of sharp scissors. You will need one large pair for cutting fabric, one small pair for cutting threads and another pair for cutting paper. It is not a good idea to use any pair other than the one you allocate for cutting paper, as the blades can become blunt quite rapidly. When you choose scissors for thread and fabric ensure that they cut to the tips and that the joint does not loosen easily.

Needles

You will need two kinds of needles: first of all blunt-ended cross stitch or tapestry needles and secondly sharp-ended crewel needles. Blunt-ended cross stitch needles are ideal for embroidering fabric with a low count and sharp-ended crewel needles are suitable for fabric with a high count. Crewel needles are also necessary for 'finishing' the end of each thread. This finishing process is achieved by threading or 'weaving' the needle through the back of the last few stitches just embroidered. All needle sizes should correspond with the type and count of the fabric being used. Refer to the guide shown at the bottom of the page to help you with each individual project. The guide also indicates how many strands of the appropriate thread should be used for each count of fabric used in the projects in this book.

Thread Organiser

There are quite a number of sophisticated thread organisers available for purchase. However, it is just as easy make your own by cutting holes in some card and looping lengths of thread through each hole. Distinguish the threads by writing the number of the thread above each hole and even the relevant symbol from the black-and-white chart.

Stranded Threads				
Fabric	Count	Needle Type	Size	Number of stranded threads
Aida	11	Tapestry	24	3
Aida	14	Tapestry	24	2
Aida	16	Tapestry	26	2
Aida	18	Tapestry	26	2
Aida	20	Tapestry	26	2
Aida	22	Crewel	8	1
Evenweave	24	Crewel	10	1
Canvas	12	Tapestry	20	Tapestry Wool

Embroidery Hoops and Frames

All cross stitch embroideries look fresh and competently done if they are kept flat throughout the time they are being stitched. This is achieved by attaching the fabric to a hoop or frame.

Embroidery Hoops

An embroidery hoop will be suitable for all of the smaller subsidiary projects in this book. The size should be large enough so that the whole design fits easily into it. If the hoop has to be moved onto existing stitches there is a danger that these will be flattened and even distorted by the pressure of the hoop. You will need to bind each hoop separately with either tape, ribbon or bias binding so that the fabric on which you stitch does not slacken (see page 15).

Rectangular Wooden Frames

The simplest form of wooden frame is known as the stretcher frame and can be purchased from most needlecraft shops. It is made by joining four narrow pieces of wood to form a rectangle. However, the joints can work loose and will prevent the fabric from remaining secure and straight, therefore exercise caution!

An alternative frame is the one that many artists use to stretch their canvas on. It is also made from lengths of wood. However, with this frame the lengths of wood have been chamfered and specially jointed at each mitred corner which fits tightly and does not loosen. They are available at well stocked art shops.

The most inexpensive way to obtain a frame, however, is to make one yourself, with the possible help of your local timber merchant. Purchase an off-cut of rectangular plywood. Mark a margin on all four edges approximately 3 cm (1 in) wide. Remove the inner rectangle with a jigsaw. Sand the outer and inner edges of the remaining wood. This has now become your frame whose main advantage is that it has no joints and therefore will never loosen.

The fabric can simply be attached with drawing pins to any of the wooden frames above. Once again it is important to ensure that the inner dimensions of your chosen frame are large enough to encompass the entire design which you are about to embroider.

Roller Frame

The roller frame is sometimes called a tapestry frame and is an essential piece of equipment for each of the large projects in this book. The advantage of this frame is that its size is adjustable. It consists of two upright bars into which are slotted two horizontal roller bars above and below. Attached to the roller bars is strong tape, which should face inwards when you assemble the frame. It is onto the tape that the fabric for embroidering is fixed. This procedure for 'dressing the frame' is described in detail on pages 14-15.

If you become addicted to cross stitch and find yourself devoting many hours to this activity, you will need a floor standing frame. There are many kinds of floor-standing frames which vary in price. Their main advantage is that both your hands are left free to embroider. Furthermore, a lamp and magnifier can be accommodated, as well as other accessories such as thread organisers, magnets, needles, scissors and chart holders, which can all be attached to the frame in various ways. It is very helpful to keep all such equipment in one place.

Pillow Case

It is essential to keep your embroidery clean. When you are not stitching, it is advisable to cover your work. If the piece is small, simply put it into a pillow case. Otherwise simply lay the pillow case or a clean cloth over the embroidery. Should your embroidery become dirty or marked, clean it using a damp cloth with a small amount of liquid soap cleaner, such as you might use to clean woollen fabric and remove any blemishes very carefully.

OPTIONAL EQUIPMENT

The following equipment, although not essential, can be useful to facilitate the cross stitch techniques.

Daylight Bulbs

These are favoured by embroiderers who stitch at night or on dull days. They can be fitted into most lamps.

Magnifiers

These are very useful for those of us with failing eyesight. They vary from small eye glasses to large floor standing magnifiers with built-in lamps. There are also line magnifiers which can be placed over the chart and facilitate each line's visibility.

Chart Holder

This keeps the chart secured with magnet strips and can be fixed to a floor standing frame so that the chart is permanently held in front of you. Because the holder itself is a magnetic board you can place a line magnifier on your chart more easily. You can even keep your spare needles on the edges of the chart holder.

Magnets

Small magnets sewn around the edges of your fabric is a useful way of holding your needles if you are using more than one thread at a time.

Marker Pens

An alternative way of indicating the edges and central lines of your embroidery than tacking with thread is to use a marker pen. Water-soluble and permanent varieties are available.

A coloured marker pen can be used on a black-and-white chart to indicate the areas you have just stitched in your embroidery. This helps you to monitor your present position and to plan how to proceed. However, ensure that you are completely satisfied that your stitches really are correct before you mark the chart, otherwise subsequent unpicking may cause confusion.

Unpicking Scissors

These are designed with a small sharp hook at the tip of the lower blade which is very useful for removing erroneous stitches.

Needle Threaders

These are very helpful for those of us with impaired eyesight and for when there is no one immediately at hand to thread the needle for us.

Shade Cards

These are available from most thread manufacturers and are useful for those of you who progress to choose alternative colours for the projects in this book and who wish to proceed to make and chart your own designs.

Graph Paper

Graph paper and tracing paper will be useful for those of you who want to make and chart your own designs. The squares of the graph paper are formed in groups which help you 'read' your colours or symbols more easily.

Small Screwdriver

A small screwdriver of the kind sometimes provided with sewing machine equipment is a useful tool for tightening the screw on the outer ring of the embroidery hoop (see page 14).

TECHNIQUES

This section describes the traditional and the well tried techniques for cross stitch in preparation, procedure and execution. Those of you who are just starting will find these suggestions – kindly offered from experts – invaluable.

Preparing the Fabric

It is not necessary to wash any of the fabric for the cross stitch projects in this book. Firstly, measure the fabric so that it is at least 6 cm (2½ in) larger on all four sides than the design and then cut the fabric out. Secondly, bind the raw edges before you actually start embroidering. Do this by either overcasting the edges with an overlocker machine or zig-zagging them with a domestic sewing machine. Alternatively, you can blanket stitch them by hand or bind them with tape, bias binding or ribbon. Each one of these methods will prevent the fabric from fraying.

Preparing the Embroidery Hoop

An embroidery hoop consists of two rings which fit into each other. The wooden varieties have a screw attached to the larger outer ring and tightening the screw ensures that the fabric is held firmly between both of the rings. In order to prevent the fabric slipping it is advisable to bind at least the inner ring with tape, bias binding or cotton ribbon and secure with a few stitches.

Some embroiderers prefer to bind both of the rings to prevent the fabric from being marked. If you do this, remember to bind both of the rings separately!

Firstly place the fabric over the inner ring and then push the outer ring around it. Check that the screw on the outer ring is at the top and in the centre of your design in order to prevent any threads catching on it when you are actually embroidering. Also make a point of ensuring that the fabric is straight and as tight as a drum, which will facilitate the cross stitch process. Use a small screwdriver to give the final twist to the screw on the outer ring of the hoop to ensure a firm grip (see Figs. 1 and 2).

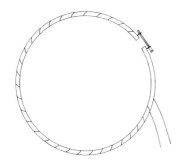

Fig. 1
Binding the outer ring of the hoop.

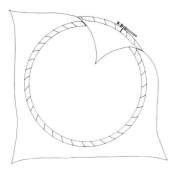

Fig. 2
Placing the fabric into the hoop.

Although it is important to ensure that the inner dimensions of your hoop are large enough to encompass the entire design, this may not always be possible. If you really must use a hoop which is smaller than the design, loosen the rings of the hoop every hour and allow the fabric to rest. Smooth out any distortions, which will probably have been caused by the hoop's pressure.

Preparing the Stretcher Frame

The frame itself needs no preparation. However, the way you attach the fabric to the frame is important. Before you begin, ensure that the whole design will fit inside the frame. Use either staples or, preferably, drawing pins to secure the fabric to the frame. Fix all four edges of the fabric to all four outer edges of the frame. Start by fixing the centre of each edge of the fabric to the centre of each side of the frame, making sure that the fabric is straight as you do this. Then fix the remaining edges of the fabric to the outer edges of the frame with your staples or drawing pins proceeding gradually from the centre to all four corners. Take care that the fabric is straight and square to the frame all the while until the fabric becomes as tight as a drum.

If you decide to use an artist's canvas frame, proceed in exactly the same way. If, however, you decide to use a home-made plywood frame, you will need to fix the edges of the fabric

to either the front or reverse sides of this frame. You may find that the points of your staples or pins may protrude if your plywood is very thin. If this happens, clip off these points with wire cutters, otherwise you may injure yourself!

Dressing the Roller Frame

It is worthwhile devoting some time to this task if you are going to spend several months embroidering a complex project. Start by making sure that the frame you purchase is wider than your fabric so that tension can be achieved at the sides as well as at the upper and lower edges. When you purchase a frame, its measurement refers to the length of the tape attached to the two roller bars.

Method

1. Assemble the frame by slotting the two horizontal roller bars (above and below) into the two vertically upright bars. Ensure that the tape attached to each roller bar faces inwards.

2. Lay the assembled rectangular frame on a table and place the fabric over the frame so that the edges of the shorter sides will be stitched to the tape on the two roller bars. Strengthen one of these edges by turning it under 1.5 cm (½ in) and stitch it to the tape of the top roller bar with either a running or hem stitch.

3. Start at the centre and stitch to the right corner and then proceed again from the centre to the left corner. This ensures the appropriate positioning of the fabric to the tape.

4. Turn the frame around laterally and stitch the other shorter edge to the tape of the bottom roller bar using exactly the same procedure.

5. Twist the top roller until about 6 cm (2½ in) of fabric is wound around it. Twist the bottom roller bar until enough fabric is wound to make the remaining fabric visible between each of the roller bars both straight and taught. Secure by tightening the wing nuts.

6. Lace each of the side edges of the fabric between the roller bars to the appropriate sides of the frame. Use a strong thread and make stitches about 2.5 cm (1 in) apart. Thus you achieve maximum tension to the fabric (see Figs. 3 and 4).

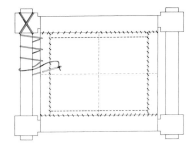

Fig. 3
Dressing the frame.

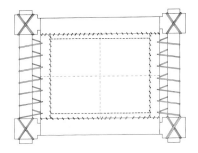

Fig. 4
The dressed frame.

7. With a long design which is not fully visible between the top and bottom roller bars, you will need to roll extra fabric into the visible area when you want to work on it. Do this by cutting the lacing threads, winding the appropriate amount of fabric into the visible area and re-lacing. In order to prevent your existing stitches crushing, insert a sheet of tissue paper between the back of the fabric and the top roller bar just before winding.

Although the frame should always be wider than the fabric, you may find that in some of the smaller projects, the fabric required is shorter than the length on the frame. You can solve this problem in two ways. Firstly, extend the length of the fabric by sewing two strips of calico, one to each of its upper and lower edges. Then attach the calico strips to the tape on the roller bars. Both ends need this preparation to ensure evenness of tension. Secondly, be extravagant with the fabric so that both upper and lower edges reach the tape on the roller bars.

Preparing the Limits of the Design

It is enormously helpful to mark the outer edges of your design with either a marker pen or, preferably, long tacking stitches with sewing thread. Many embroiderers also like to mark the central lines of the design both horizontally and vertically. Traditionally, it is usual to begin stitching a cross stitch embroidery at the centre. However, a number of embroiderers prefer to begin at either the top of the design and work towards the bottom or vice versa, particularly if the design is a complex one. It is a very personal choice. Note that when embroidering long designs, these necessitate rolling the fabric during the course of your chosen project. In this case you will need to decide at the start which system you use so that you roll the extra fabric around the appropriate top or bottom roller bar.

Threading the Needle

This may seem a most basic and maybe an unnecessary procedure to mention. However it is included here quite simply because of all the complaints picked up from embroidery friends, 'I can't thread my needle!' is by far the most commonly heard.

There are three ways to thread a needle which makes this procedure less problematic:

• Bend the thread around the eye of the needle, making a loop. Grip tightly between the thumb and finger of one hand so that the needle's eye and thread are hidden. Carefully slide out the needle and push its eye onto and around the loop which has been formed. This is more successful than pushing the thread through the eye of the needle (see Fig. 5).

Fig. 5
Threading the needle with folded end of thread.

• Fold a tiny piece of firm but fine paper over the end of the thread which is then easier to insert through the eye of the needle (see Fig. 6).

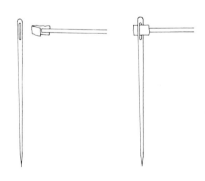

Fig. 6
Threading the needle with paper over the folded thread.

• Use a needle threader – this works on the principle that it is easier to push the needle's eye around wire than thread. Self-threading needles are also available for those of us who should have bought a new pair of spectacles! (see Fig. 7.)

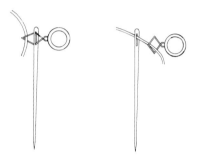

Fig. 7
Using the needle threader.

You may have noticed that there has been no mention of licking the end of the thread, closing one eye and sticking out the tongue in a vain attempt to push a damp end of thread through the eye of a needle. However, if you really must thread your needle in this way, cut off the damp end afterwards!

The Stitches

There are two ways to create crosses to form all the projects in this book (see Figs. 8, 9 and 10). One way is to form each cross individually. The other way is to form half crosses (petit point) and return later with the same thread to complete the full cross (gros point). Either way, all the initial, half cross stitches should lie in one and the same direction and the second full cross stitches should do the same, but in the

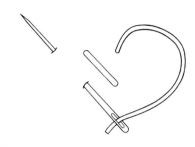

Fig. 8
Full cross stitch formed individually (gros point).

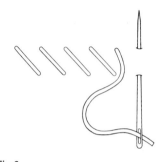

Fig. 9
First stage of a row of cross stitch (otherwise known as half cross stitch or petit point).

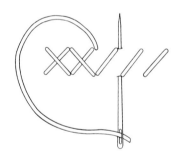

Fig. 10
Second stage completing a row of full cross stitch (gros point).

opposite direction to the first.

Most of the projects in this book are designed in such a way that colours change frequently from cross to cross. If you look at both the colour and black-and-white charts you will see this is so by the way the coloured squares and symbols interchange frequently. This 'pointillistic' approach is intended to reinstate the exalted heritage of opus pulvinarium (the term used for examples of cross stitch found in the Middle Ages) where three dimensional forms can be portrayed by subtle juxtaposition of colours and tones without resorting to outlining with back stitch. It is for this reason that the forming of a full cross individually will be the most satisfactory way to embroider most areas of all the projects. Only when there is an area which is composed of one colour is it possible to form half crosses in rows and return later to complete the full cross.

Method

1. Start by knotting the thread, and then pass the threaded needle from the front to the back of the fabric just outside the design. Make your first stitches a little way into the design. Eventually you will stitch towards the edge of the design with the appropriately coloured thread as your chart directs. If you start each thread in this way, in effect, all the threads will have been couched on the back of the fabric. Eventually all the knots can be cut and the trailing threads at the back of the fabric can be safely trimmed.

2. There are four actions required to form a full cross stitch. Firstly, identify four holes which will be the four points of the cross and bring the needle from the back of the fabric through the bottom left hole. Secondly, pass the needle through the top right hole from the front to

the back of the fabric so that the thread forms its first half cross at a 45 degree angle. Thirdly, bring the needle up through the bottom right hole and fourthly, down through the top left hole. This is one full cross stitch.

3. Continue to make crosses until you nearly come to the end of the thread. Finish by passing the needle through the last few stitches on the back of the fabric. This secures the thread neatly and efficiently.

It is traditional to use a dark-toned thread to begin making stitches which act as reference points for subsequent stitching. However, some embroiderers like to have a number of threads all in separate needles so that they may stitch the threads concurrently either line by line or area by area. This is a matter of preference.

Reading the Charts

Both colour and black-and-white charts for every project are shown within each chapter so that you can decide which is preferable for your way of working. The colour charts can be used more easily if you divide them into squares of 10 x 10 stitches each. This can be done by superimposing a transparent grid over the chart. It makes the chart simple to follow and counting is then kept to a minimum.

The black-and-white charts, shown within each chapter, can be enlarged on a photocopying machine, which will make the symbols clearer to follow.

Framing, Mounting and Lacing the Finished Embroidery

First of all, consult your local picture framer and decide what kind of frame you would like. Also decide whether or not you want a mount; it is advisable to have one if you choose to glaze the embroidery because the pressure of glass will flatten the stitches. The choice of frame and mount is very personal. However, try to choose ones which enhance rather than dominate the embroidery. Generally, it is a good idea to choose a frame which will fit with those that you may already have hanging on your walls but which is also well suited to the embroidery. Should you decide to have a mount, the embroidery looks more effective if the colour of the mount is subdued and similar to one of the main threads you have used.

Method

1. Select some stiff, rigid and acid-free card or even some thin board which should either be laminated or sealed in some way. This is because acids from wood pulp will, in time, stain and eventually destroy your embroidery. Cut the card or board to the same shape and size of the inner dimensions of the frame allowing the necessary extra few millimetres (approx $\frac{1}{8}$ in) of the recess at the back of the frame. Remember to check with your picture framer about these extra dimensions.

2. Lay the embroidery face downwards on a damp towel and press with a moderately hot iron until the fabric and embroidery are smooth and flat.

3. Lay the embroidery face downwards onto a clean flat surface with the acid free card or laminated board on top, ensuring that the embroidery is centred. If you have decided to have a mount for the embroidery, centre the embroidery so that the dimensions of the margins of the surrounding fabric correspond to those of the mount.

4. Fold over two opposite edges of the fabric and make mitred folds at the corners. Lace across them using strong thread. Repeat this process for the other two opposite edges

until the embroidery is tightly stretched over the card or board. Keep checking that the embroidery is centred and that the weave of the fabric is straight and parallel to the edges of the card or board.

5. Finally, stitch the mitred edges until they are neat and secure (see Figs. 11 and 12).

This procedure is suitable for all of the main projects in this book. Directions for making up or assembling the second projects for each design are given at the end of each chapter where appropriate. Many of these projects are mounted in small household items which you can obtain from a needlework supplier (see List of Suppliers, page 143). Instructions for mounting

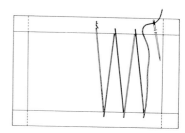

Fig. 11
Lacing the finished embroidery.

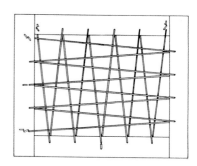

Fig. 12
The laced embroidery.

your embroidery onto the items are provided by the supplier.

CHAPTER 2

FELES, THE SAMPLER*

Size: 25 x 38 cm (10 x 15 in)
Embroidered by Kitty Mogford

As for words, they define less than the house cat illustrates them:
aesthetic, sublime, tragic, comic,
symmetry, supremacy, dignity, charm and grace;
in short, the beautiful.

From *Honorable Cat* by Paul Gallico (1897–1976)

'Feles' is the name given to the cat genus from which the entire cat tribe originates. The word come from the Latin, felinus, meaning a cat; the plural, feles from which we get the adjective, feline, pertains to all cat kind. This sampler was originally a test piece of embroidery and depicts six simplified faces of cats that will appear again in more complex forms as subsequent projects. Original samplers often feature a text; here there is a statement by Colette, 'there are no ordinary cats', a sentiment with which, as cat lovers, I am sure you will agree.

DESIGN CONSIDERATIONS

Art in harmony, harmony is the analogy of contraries and the analogy of similarities, of line, of colour and of tone.

Georges Seurat (1859–1891)

Design considerations are as much an important part of this book as are materials and techniques. We all need to band together to help close the conflicting divide between artists and craftsmen and women. Hence I chose the artist Georges Seurat, who was as much a craftsman as he was an artist, to provide us with the key to creative harmonious design. Throughout this book most projects will refer to the precepts which imbue his statement. You will deepen your understanding of how 'contraries' or contrasting elements, together with 'similarities' or similar elements, are essential ingredients for the creation of harmony in a design.

'Contraries' create effects which are lively, animating, exciting and even surprising; if too many 'contrasts' exist then chaos and anarchy reign. 'Similarities' or the repetition of similar elements create effects which blend, merge, unify and integrate; if too many 'similarities' exist uniformity and tedium reign.

The colours in this sampler contrast with each other in two different ways. Firstly, they contrast in 'hue' as some of the colours verge towards orange and one of the other colours is blue. Orange and blue are known as a complementary pair of colours. There is also one green and one pale pink (which is a pale tone of red). Red and green are also complementary colours. The third pair is purple and yellow, which you will encounter in a subsequent project. Any complementary pair of colours will produce a contrasting and lively effect. Secondly, the colours contrast in tone. The tonal values of the colours range from quite dark to very pale. This contrast similarly produces a lively effect. At the same time these hues and tones of colour are dispersed throughout the design in order to unify the composition by repetition. The same is true for the 'line' which we can interpret here as direction. Your eyes will follow the colour hues and tones around an implied oval into which you will stitch the text which is an obvious contrast to the representation of the cats. However, because the text will be stitched in one of the colours present elsewhere, a blending, merging and unifying effect will be achieved, preventing the text from appearing too dominant. Thus, as well as using this sampler to try your stitch technique, you will at the same time be using it to consider some fundamental aspects of design.

MATERIALS

Threads				
Sranded Cottons	**DMC**	**Anchor**	**Madeira**	**Skeins**
Tan very light	739	366	2013	1
Cream	712	926	1908	1
Tan light	738	361	2013	1
Sea Foam Green – medium light	3813	875	1702	1
Terracotta very light	3779	868	0403	1
Baby Blue Ultra – very light	3756	1037	2504	1

Aida, 14 count, 50 x 60 cm (20 x 23½ in).

Tapestry needle, size 24

Roller (or 'tapestry') frame, wider than the width of aida

Strong sewing thread

METHOD

1. Prepare the fabric and dress the frame (see pages 14–16), ensuring that the fabric is as tight as possible.

2. Tack the border and central lines, from top to bottom and from side to side of the design. This creates clear guidelines for embroidering.

3. Because the design is asymmetrical and composed of only six coloured threads, you may find it simpler to embroider the darkest colours first and progress to the palest colours last.

4. Once completed, lace, mount and frame the embroidery (see pages 18–19).

KEY

Tan very light
Cream
Tan light
Sea Foam Green medium light
Terracotta very light
Baby Blue Ultra very light

Stitch count: 149 x 210

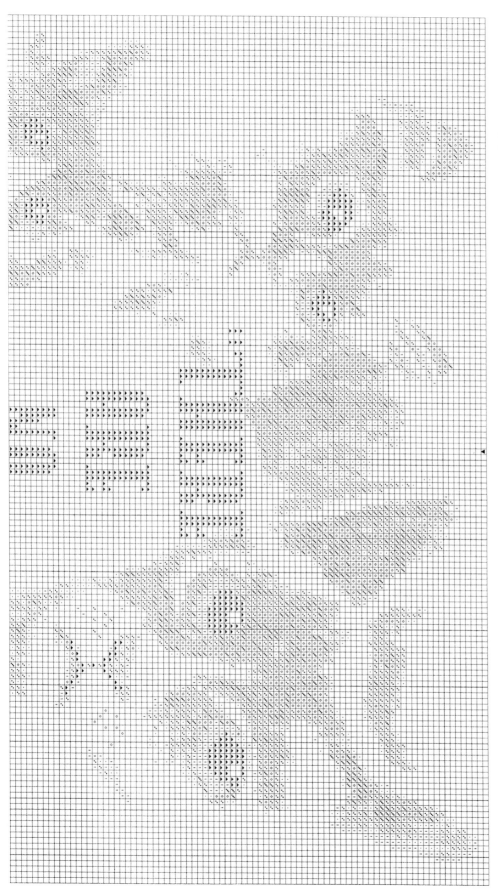

KEY

- ▪ Tan very light
- · Cream
- ◇ Tan light
- ▲ Sea Foam Green medium light
- ▪ Terracotta very light
- ! Baby Blue Ultra very light

Stitch count: 149 x 210

CHAPTER 3
FREYA, THE NORWEGIAN FOREST CAT **

Size 27 x 35 cm (10¼ x 13¾ in)
Embroidered by Bernice Brown

Refined and delicate natures understand the cat. Women poets,

and artists hold it in great esteem…indeed, only coarse natures fail to

discern the natural distinction of the cat.

From *Le Chats* (1885)

by Jules Husson Champfleury (1821–1889)

FREYA, THE NORWEGIAN FOREST CAT

This active, athletic and naturally distinctive cat gives the impression of great power and fortitude. It is said that, long ago, this large and fearsome cat of the northern forests was taken by the Vikings to guard their homes, to live alongside their families as hunters and household pets. In Norse mythology the chariot of Freya, Goddess of Beauty, Youth, Love and Fertility, was drawn by two such long-haired cats who were imbued not only with strength but also with creativity. They were also pleasure-loving and ease-seeking in between bouts of energetic activity.

DESIGN CONSIDERATIONS

If contrast is needed, let it be used as the means of rendering the whole more powerful, brilliant and striking. For instance, if orange is intended to predominate … let blue be mingled with it, but sparingly.

From *Art in Ornament and Dress* by Charles Blanc (1873)

You have already discovered that contrast is a useful way of producing strong effects. Freya needs this contrast in order to portray her character. However, the effect also needs to be pleasurable. 'Let the complementary colour be its auxiliary, and not its rival' continues Charles Blanc. You will notice that only a few blues are used, and sparingly, in order to enhance, and not to wage war with, the predominant amounts of orange and warm browns.

MATERIALS

Aida, 14 count, 43 x 48 cm (17 x 19 in)
Tapestry needle, size 24
Roller (or 'tapestry') frame, wider than the fabric width
Strong sewing thread

Threads									
Sranded Cottons	DMC	Anchor	Madeira	Skeins	Sranded Cottons	DMC	Anchor	Madeira	Skeins
Cream	712	926	1908	4	Sky Blue very light	747	158	1101	1
Old Gold very light	677	886	2207	2	White	Blanc	2	2402	1
Gold	783	307	2514	2	Golden Yellow very light	3078	292	0102	1
Yellow medium	743	305	0109	2	Beige Brown light	841	378	2601	1
Drab Brown light	613	853	2110	1	Mocha Brown medium dark	3032	832	2002	1
Brown Grey light	3023	392	1906	1	Orange Spice light	722	323	0307	1
Antique Mauve medium	316	1017	0809	1	Shell Grey dark	451	233	1808	1
Baby Blue medium light	3755	140	0910	1	Lemon light	445	288	0103	1
White bright	B5200	1	2401	1	Antique Blue medium	931	1034	1711	1

METHOD

1. Prepare the aida, dress the frame (see pages 14–16) and mark the border and central lines of the design.

2. Embroider in full cross stitch. It is advisable to embroider the many large areas of single colour in their entirety using the lengths of the appropriately coloured thread. Avoid moving to another part of the design requiring the same coloured thread immediately, because this may distort the tension. Embroider each different coloured area consecutively in order to achieve an even tension.

3. Once completed, lace, mount and frame the embroidery (see pages 18–19).

FREYA'S HEAD (CALENDAR) **

Size: 20 x 21 cm (8 x 8¼ in)
Embroidered by Gill Brown
(detail only shown)

Cats know how to obtain food without labour, shelter
without confinement and love without penalties.
Walter Lionel George (1882–1926)

DESIGN CONSIDERATIONS

Freyia, thin robed, about her ankles slim
The grey cats playing.

From *Lovers of Gudrun* by William Morris (1834–96)

The Goddess Freya, like our cat, was not only a pleasure loving, ease-seeking being but also, when aroused, could be as energetic as her cats and, indeed, even don her armour and lead her step-daughters, the Valkyries, to the battlefield. It is said that on such occasions her cats turned 'grimalkin', a name given to cats of a grey colour in medieval times. For this reason Freya's head is designed in many tones of grey. However, in order to enliven a possible uniformity or even tedium, touches of pale yellow, dark blue and violet are included. This colour can be used to produce certain effects which directly relate to and embody the purpose of the design.

MATERIALS

Aida, 14 Count, 30 x 45 cm (12 x 13¾ in)
Tapestry needle, size 24
Roller (or 'tapestry') frame, wider than the fabric width
Strong sewing thread

METHOD

1. Prepare the aida, dress the frame (see pages 14–16) and mark out the border and central lines of the embroidery.

2. Embroider in full cross stitch.

3. When the embroidery is finished, press if necessary and lace it onto stiff card or laminated board, as described on pages 18–19. Attach a calendar to its lower edge and a cord to its upper edge and hang in position.

Threads

Sranded Cottons	DMC	Anchor	Madeira	Skeins	Sranded Cottons	DMC	Anchor	Madeira	Skeins
Beige Grey light	822	390	1908	1	Grey Green light	927	848	1708	1
Pearl Grey very light	762	234	1709	1	Sea Foam Green				
White bright	B5200	1	2401	1	medium light	3813	875	1702	1
Grey Green very light	928	274	1708	1	Steel Grey light	318	399	1802	1
Pearl Grey	415	398	1802	1	Beaver Grey light	648	900	1709	1
Beaver Grey very light	3072	847	1805	1	Grey Green medium	926	850	1707	1
Antique Violet very light	3743	869	2611	1	Beaver Grey medium	647	1040	1813	1
Antique Blue light	932	1033	1711	1	Steel Grey dark	414	235	1801	1

When I play with my cat, who knows whether she is not
rather amusing herself with me than I with her.

Michel de Montaigne (1533–1592)

KEY

for main project

Cream
Old Gold very light
Gold
Yellow medium
Drab Brown light
Brown Grey light
Antique Mauve medium
Baby Blue medium light
White bright
Sky Blue very light
White
Golden Yellow very light
Beige Brown light
Mocha Brown medium dark
Orange Spice light
Shell Grey dark
Lemon light
Antique Blue medium

Stitch count: 151 x 187

KEY

for calendar

Beige Grey light

Pearl Grey very light

White bright

Grey Green very light

Pearl Grey

Beaver Grey very light

Antique Violet very light

Antique Blue light

Grey Green light

Sea Foam Green medium light

Steel Grey light

Beaver Grey light

Grey Green medium

Beaver Grey medium

Steel Grey dark

Stitch count: 123 x 115

KEY

for calendar

! Beige Grey light

∧ Pearl Grey very light

· White bright

− Grey Green very light

∧ Pearl Grey

✗ Beaver Grey very light

∅ Antique Violet very light

⋮ Antique Blue light

✕ Grey Green light

↑ Sea Foam Green medium light

⋰ Steel Grey light

║ Beaver Grey light

☐ Grey Green medium

✖ Beaver Grey medium

◉ Steel Grey dark

Stitch count: 123 x 115

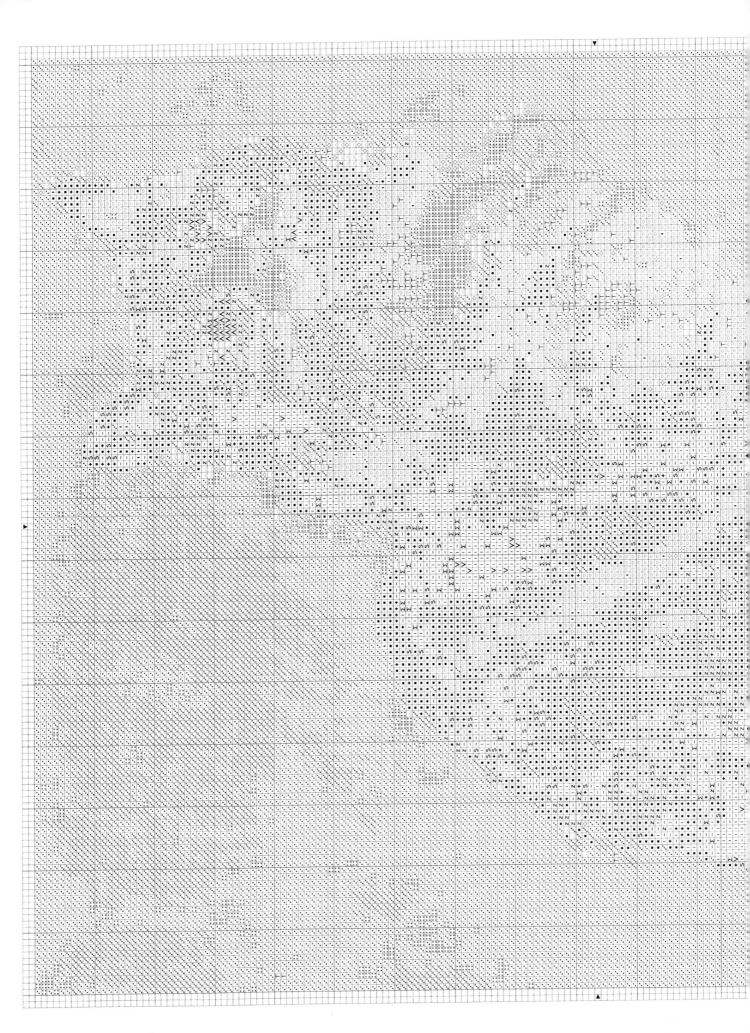

CHAPTER 4
OTTO, THE TURKISH VAN **

Size: 26 x 34 cm (10 x 13³⁄₈ in)
Embroidered by Jennie Hubbard

The cat is the animal to whom the Creator has the biggest
eye, the softest fur, the most supremely delicate nostrils,
a mobile ear, an unrivalled paw and a
curved claw borrowed from a rose tree ...

Colette (1873–1954)

The Turkish Van evolves within the Angora breed. All cats of this kind are much admired for their quiet, graceful charm and for their long, silky coats which are white with an attractive auburn colouring in their ears and tails. Living high in the mountainous regions of Lake Van they have always been uniquely expert swimmers, earning the name of 'swimming cats' in Turkey. This cat is named 'Otto', after the Ottoman Empire.

DESIGN CONSIDERATIONS

There is no art delivered to mankind that hath not the works of nature for his principle object.
Sir Philip Sidney (1554–1586)

There is a natural phenomenon called 'simultaneous contrast' where a complementary colour appears in areas of grey close to bright colours. This curious optical illusion will now appear before your eyes if you concentrate on the bright orange area in Otto's ears or tail. The grey shadows in his white fur will appear slightly blue in your peripheral vision. In order to augment this illusion, blue is deliberately included with the grey. Along with the blue of the stairs, this enhances the orange. This is an example of how a contrast of differences enlivens the composition.

MATERIALS
Aida, 14 count, 50 x 60 cm (20 x 24 in)
Tapestry needle, size 24
Roller (or 'tapestry') frame, wider than the fabric width
Strong sewing thread

METHOD

1. Prepare the aida, dress the frame (see pages 14–16) and mark the border and central lines of the design.

2. Embroider in full cross stitch using two strands of thread throughout.

3. Once completed, lace, mount and frame the embroidery (see pages 18–19).

Threads				
Sranded Cottons	**DMC**	**Anchor**	**Madeira**	**Skeins**
Cornflower Blue medium dark	3807	122	2702	4
Baby Blue medium light	3755	140	1013	2
Cornflower Blue medium	793	176	0906	2
White bright	B5200	1	2401	1
Ecru	Ecrut	387	2404	1
Pearl Grey very light	762	234	1804	1
Tan medium light	437	362	2012	1
Antique Blue very light	3752	1032	0908	1
Beige Brown light	841	378	2601	1
Terracotta medium light	3778	1013	2310	1
Grey Green very light	928	274	1708	1
Shell Grey dark	451	233	1808	1
Antique Violet very light	3743	869	2611	1
Antique Blue light	932	1033	1710	1
Delft Blue medium	799	136	0910	1
Steel Grey light	318	399	1802	1
Beige Brown very light	842	376	1910	1
Yellow Beige light	3047	852	2205	1
Baby Blue very light	755	128	1001	1
Pearl Grey	415	398	1802	1
Drab Brown light	613	853	2109	1
Orange Spice very light	402	1047	2307	1
Sportsman Flesh	945	881	2309	1
Yellow very light	745	300	0111	1

OTTO'S HEAD (GREETING CARD) *

Size of aperture: 9.5 x 14 cm (3¾ x 5½ in)
Embroidered by Elizabeth Hadwick

I love cats because I love my home and after a
while they become its visible soul.

Jean Cocteau (1889–1963)

DESIGN CONSIDERATIONS

Less is more.

Ludwig Mies Van De Rohe (1886–1969)

The design for this card is composed in the same colour scheme as the main project. However, there are considerably less threads with which to embroider it. Sometimes the employment of 'less' produces a 'more' striking effect. Nevertheless, orange is again an auxiliary rather than a rival to blue, as the intention is to create a design both powerful and harmonious; Otto does not need to be rendered conspicuous as much as he needs to be admired.

MATERIALS

Aida, 16 count, 15 x 23 cm (6 x 9 in)

Tapestry needle, size 26

Embroidery hoop or rectangular wooden frame, larger than the design but smaller than the dimensions of the aida

Strong sewing thread

Greetings card with rectangular aperture of 9.5 x 14 cm (3¼ x 5½ in)

Threads									
Sranded Cottons	DMC	Anchor	Madeira	Skeins	Sranded Cottons	DMC	Anchor	Madeira	Skeins
Cornflower Blue					Baby Blue very light	775	128	1001	1
medium dark	3807	122	2702	2	Baby Blue light	3325	129	1002	1
Cream	712	926	2101	1	Pearl Grey	415	398	1802	1
Delft medium	799	136	0910	1	White	Blanc	2	2402	1
Steel Grey light	318	399	1802	1	Drab Brown light	613	853	2109	1
Beige Brown very light	842	376	1910	1	Orange Spice very light	402	1047	2307	1
Yellow Beige light	3047	852	2205	1					

METHOD

1. Prepare the aida and the hoop or wooden frame (see pages 14–15). Mark out the border and central lines.

2. Embroider in full cross stitch. These designs have quite large areas of one colour, so you may like to embroider these areas in the way described on page 29 for 'Freya'. Start embroidering either at the top, the bottom or the middle of the design – the choice is yours.

3. When you have finished the embroidery, follow the next set of instructions to frame it with the greetings card.

FRAMING THE EMBROIDERY WITH THE GREETINGS CARD
Method

1. Open the three panels of your greetings card and place the opened card face downwards onto a clean surface.

2. Remove the embroidery from the embroidery hoop or frame. If necessary, press the embroidery so that it looks fresh.

3. Trim the fabric so that its dimensions are slightly smaller than those of the fully folded card and so that the embroidery fits the aperture.

4. Run a fine line of fabric adhesive around the aperture on the inside of the card but not too near the edge. Place the fabric onto the surface with the embroidery facing upwards.

5. Check which way the card is to open and gently lower the card, glue side down, onto the fabric so that the embroidery is centrally placed within the aperture.

6. Turn the card over so that the reverse side of the embroidery is facing you. Run another fine line of adhesive within the outer edges of the left panel and fold onto the reverse side of the embroidery. Smooth the two joining panels to secure and finish the card.

KEY
for main project

- Cornflower Blue medium dark
- Baby Blue medium light
- Cornflower Blue medium
- White bright
- Delft medium
- Pearl Grey
- Ecru
- Pearl Grey light
- Tan medium light
- Baby Blue very light
- Yellow Beige light
- Antique Blue very light
- Antique Violet very light
- Terracotta medium light
- Beige Brown very light
- Drab Brown light
- Grey Green very light
- Shell Grey dark
- Antique Violet light
- Antique Blue light
- Orange Spice very light
- Sportsman Flesh
- Steel Grey light
- Yellow very light

Stitch count: 143 X 193

KEY

for greetings card

 Cornflower Blue medium dark

Cream

Delft medium

Steel Grey light

Beige Brown very light

Yellow Beige light

Baby Blue very light

Baby Blue light

Pearl Grey

White

Drab Brown light

Orange Spice very light

Stitch count: 62 x 84

KEY

for greetings card

♥	Cornflower Blue medium dark	ز	Baby Blue very light
.	Cream	✚	Baby Blue light
I	Delft medium	人	Pearl Grey
N	Steel Grey light	—	White
+	Beige Brown very light	✦	Drab Brown light
r	Yellow Beige light	♡	Orange Spice very light

Stitch count: 62 x 84

■ Cornflower Blue medium dark
Z Baby Blue medium light
⊘ Cornflower Blue medium
· White bright
I Ecru
⁄ Pearl Grey very light
! Tan medium light
⋏ Antique Blue very light
⋌ Beige Brown light
ɔ Terracotta medium light
ⲅ Grey Green very light
⭨ Shell Grey dark
S Antique Violet very light
⸭ Antique Blue light
+ Delft Blue medium
✦ Steel Grey light
– Beige Brown very light
◣ Yellow Beige light
⊘ Baby Blue very light
⠒ Pearl Grey
♡ Drab Brown light
ɹ Orange Spice very light
N Sportsman Flesh
⠄ Yellow very light

Stitch count: 143 X 193

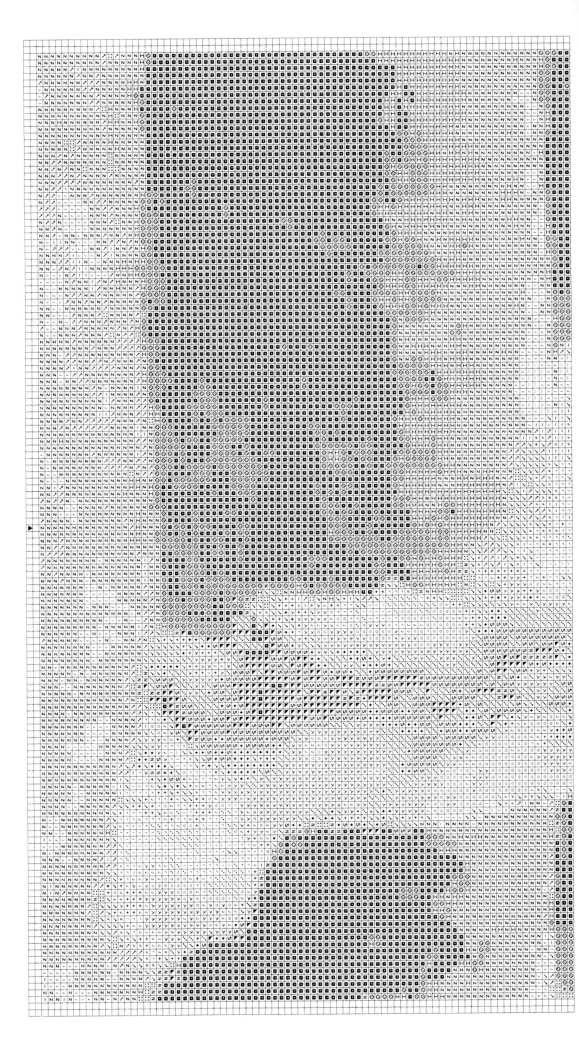

CHAPTER 5
MIA, THE SIAMESE **

Size: diameter = 34 cm (13½ in)
Embroidered by Pat Ripley

In meditation they take their noble attitudes
Of great sphinxes stretched in profound solitudes
Who seem to sleep in a dream without end.
From *Cats* by Charles Baudelaire (1821–1867)

Early Siamese cats tended to have kinked tails and squinted eyes. The legendary origin for these characteristics derives from a story about a pair of cats called Mia (mother) and Pho (father). They were sent into the jungle by some Buddhist priests to look for a priceless goblet which had been stolen from their temple. When they discovered it, Pho returned with the glad tidings while Mia remained to guard it. She was so concerned that it should never be stolen again that she wound her tail around the base of the goblet and persistently kept her eyes fixed upon it. When Pho returned with the priests they not only recovered the goblet but also discovered that Mia's tail was kinked and her eyes were squinted. Moreover, she had given birth to kittens with the same characteristics!

DESIGN CONSIDERATIONS

Brown is unemotional and disciplined.
It is outwardly inaudible but rings of a
powerful inner harmony.
Wassily Kandinsky (1896–1914)

You will remember reading in the introduction how the use of colour can produce different effects. All sensitive artists and craftsmen and women have known this and many have written about it. It is important to understand that, although the general principle is universally accepted, the specific and individual responses to particular colours may differ. For example, you may have a different response to brown than that described by Kandinsky. Indeed, it may be your desire to change the colour hues in this design completely. If you do so, remember to match the tonal values in order to preserve the naturalistic aspects of the cat and the balance of the design. Indeed, if you glance now at the subsidiary project in this chapter, you will see that blue substitutes brown. Brown is used here because my response to brown is similar to that of Kandinsky. I intend Mia to be represented as quietly watchful as well as powerfully and harmoniously steadfast, so that the colour of the whole design evokes and realises her role in the ancient legend.

MATERIALS

Threads				
Sranded Cottons	**DMC**	**Anchor**	**Madeira**	**Skeins**
Beige Grey medium	644	830	1814	4
Tan medium light	437	362	2012	4
Tan light	738	361	2013	4
Beige Brown very light	842	376	1910	3
Steel Grey light	318	399	1802	3
Antique Blue medium	931	1034	1711	3
Beige Brown light	841	378	2601	2
Beige Brown ultra very light	543	933	0306	2
Off White	746	275	0101	1

Aida, 14 count, 51 x 51 cm (20 x 20 in)

Tapestry needle, size 24

Roller (or 'tapestry') frame, wider than the width of the fabric

Strong sewing thread

METHOD

1. Prepare the aida and dress the frame as you would for a square or rectangular shaped embroidery (see pages 14–16). Mark the edge of the circular design with tacking stitches as well as the vertical and horizontal central lines.

2. Embroider in full cross stitch. You may prefer to start embroidering at the centre and proceed outwards.

3. Once completed, lace, mount and frame the embroidery. Do this by lacing the embroidery on a square sheet of stiff card or board and selecting a mount with a circular aperture (see page 42).

MIA'S HEAD (FOOTSTOOL) *

Size: diameter = 12 cm (8¼in)
Embroidered by Jessie Street

For in the stillness a cat languishes loudly. Much is she worth and even more is made of her.
Felicia Dorothea Hemans (1793–1835)

DESIGN CONSIDERATIONS

Blue is peaceful, heavenly, spiritual,
cold and moves into itself.
Wassily Kandinsky (1866–1944)

Brown is exchanged here with blue. This demonstrates how it is possible to change any colour hue of a design, so long as the tonal values are matched in order to maintain the balance of the composition. In addition, this realises other aspects of Mia's character implied in the legend. Blue is generally regarded as a cool, peaceful colour. However, in excess it can evoke negative responses. Therefore warm purples, in the form of violet and mauves, are introduced in order to redress such an extremity of reaction and this also represents Mia's animated yet disciplined role.

MATERIALS

Threads				
Sranded Cottons	**DMC**	**Anchor**	**Madeira**	**Skeins**
Off White	746	275	0101	4
Electric Blue	995	410	1102	2
Blue Violet	340	118	2711	1
Baby Blue light	3325	129	0907	1
Blue Violet light	341	117	0901	1
Delft dark	798	131	0911	1
Sky Blue very light	747	158	1101	1
Mauve very light	3609	85	0710	1
Blue Violet medium	3746	1030	2711	1

Aida, 16 count, 50 x 50 cm (19¾ x 19¾ in)
Tapestry needle, size 26
A roller (or 'tapestry') frame, wider than the fabric width
Strong sewing thread

METHOD

1. Follow the instructions for the main project on the previous page.

2. When the embroidery has been completed, press it on to a dampened cloth with a moderately hot iron until the stitches are smooth and fresh.

FITTING THE EMBROIDERY INTO THE FOOTSTOOL
Method

1. Purchase a footstool from your local needlework supplier.

2. Run a gathering thread around the edge of the design creating a margin of 6 cm (2½ in) all round.

3. Cut away all excess fabric leaving another margin of 1 cm (½ in) around the gathering thread.

4. Pull the thread tight as you place and smooth the embroidery over the footstool pad. Secure the thread with five overlapping stitches.

5. Place the pad in the stool and screw it in position from the bottom. Instructions for fitting the embroidery onto the stool will be provided by the supplier. The one illustrated here was supplied by Francesca Lawrence (see List of Suppliers, page 143).

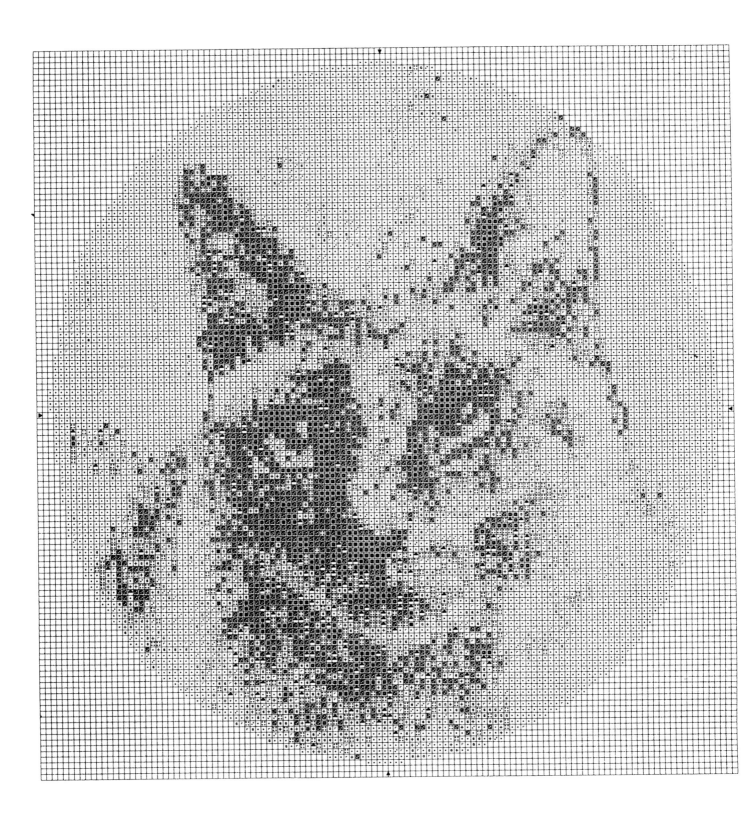

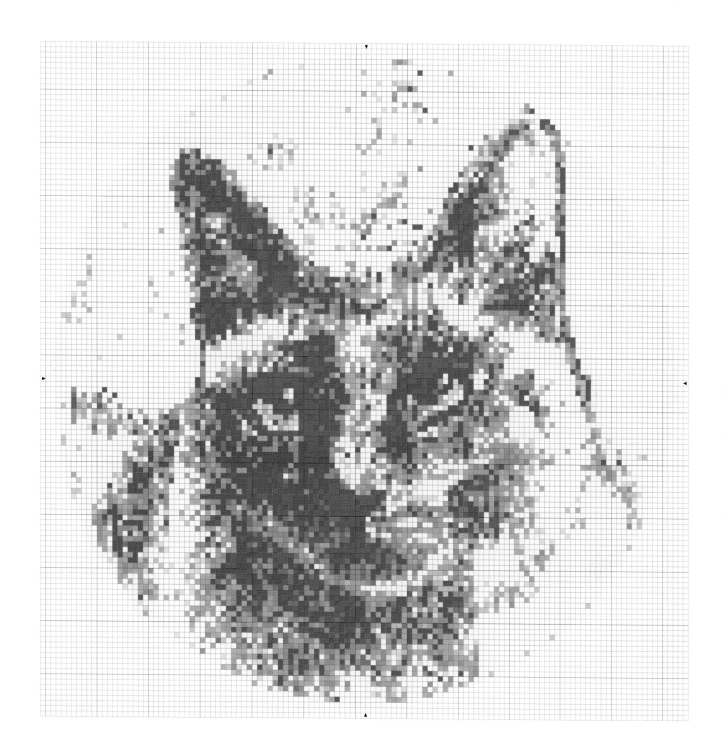

KEY

for footstool

- ·   Off White
- ◩   Electric Blue
- ⠿   Blue Violet
- ✦   Baby Blue light
- G   Blue Violet light
- ▣   Delft dark
- ▪   Sky Blue very light
- ┌   Mauve very light
- ◓   Blue Violet medium

Stitch count: 122 x 123

KEY

for footstool

	Off White
■	Electric Blue
■	Blue Violet
■	Baby Blue light
■	Blue Violet light
■	Delft dark
■	Sky Blue very light
■	Mauve very light
■	Blue Violet medium

Stitch count: 122 x 123

KEY

for main project

- Beige Grey medium
- Tan medium light
- Tan light
- Beige Brown very light
- Steel Grey light
- Antique Blue medium
- Beige Brown light
- Beige Brown ultra very light
- Off White

Stitch count: 195 X 195

KEY

for main project

◤ Beige Grey medium

✗ Tan medium light

ل Tan light

+ Beige Brown very light

⋮ Steel Grey light

◉ Antique Blue medium

S Beige Brown light

▪ Beige Brown ultra very light

· Off White

Stitch count: 195 X 195

CHAPTER 6
SI SAWAT, THE KORAT ***

Size: 45 x 35 cm (18 x 14 in)
Embroidered by Pauline Garnham

Observe the cat upon this page
Philosophers in every age,
The very wisest of the wise,
Have tried her mind to analyse
In vain, for nothing can they learn
She baffles them at every turn ...
From *The Cat* by Oliver Hereford (1863–1935)

'Si Sawat' means good fortune and was the name given to the Korats in their native country of Thailand where they were much prized for their beauty and sweet natures. There exists a collection of ancient Thai manuscripts, written between 1350 and 1767, which include descriptions of this 'blue' cat with *hairs so smooth, with roots like clouds and tips like silver and eyes that shine like dewdrops.* Occasionally, the coats of some Korats were almost indigo in hue and were known as 'black pearls.'

DESIGN CONSIDERATIONS

Now you of noble mind who love this profession be guided by these basic principles – love, respect, willingness to abide by the rules, and perseverance.

Cennino Cennini (1365–1440)

The word 'design' has many meanings. So far in this book it has been used to refer to the way that certain colour combinations can create particular effects. Such effects depend on intention. 'Design' has also been used to refer to the way that colour combinations need to be composed to create a balanced harmony. In addition to this 'Design' describes the process by which one works or travels on the journey of creativity. It refers, therefore, also to the plan or route towards the harmonious intention.

Because this is the first complex project it may help you to follow some guidelines so that you may increase your 'love' and 'respect' for cross stitch embroidery and develop your aptitude for 'perseverance' in the way that you execute this project.

Sit comfortably at your embroidery with your equipment and materials clearly visible, sensibly organised and close at hand. Create a working environment that is quiet and peaceful, without distractions. It has been said that the maximum length of time that anyone can fully concentrate on an activity is twenty minutes. After such time the mind is tired, tends to become confused and mistakes can be made. Therefore, interrupt your embroidering at regular intervals and engage in a completely different activity for five or ten minutes such as making a cup of tea or taking a short walk. There is nothing more infuriating than having to unpick erroneous stitches simply because of tiredness. However, herein lies another rule. Ignore the fury because it wastes energy. Learn from the lesson of the error. Become more willing 'to abide by the rules' and persevere.

MATERIALS

Aida, 14 count, 56 x 46 cm (22 x 18 in)
Tapestry needle, size 24
Roller (or 'tapestry') frame, wider than the fabric width
Strong sewing thread

Threads

Sranded Cottons	DMC	Anchor	Madeira	Skeins	Sranded Cottons	DMC	Anchor	Madeira	Skeins
White	Blanc	2	2402	4	Steel Grey light	318	399	1802	2
Antique Blue very light	3752	1032	0908	3	Pearl Grey very light	762	234	1709	1
Antique Blue light	932	1033	1710	2	Antique Blue medium	931	1034	1711	1
Yellow Ultra very light	3823	386	2512	2	Tan very light	739	366	2013	1
Grey green very light	928	274	1708	2	Yellow light	744	301	0112	1

SI SAWAT, THE KORAT

METHOD

1. Prepare the aida and dress the frame (see pages 14–16).
   Mark the border and central lines of the design.

2. Embroider in full cross stitch.

3. Once completed, lace, mount and frame the embroidery
   (see pages 18–19).

SI SAWAT'S HEAD (TRAY) ***

Size: 25.5 x 18.5 cm (10 x 7¼ in)
Embroidered by Beryl Bowcott

… He is a very fine cat, a very fine cat indeed!
Samuel Johnson (1709–1784)

DESIGN CONSIDERATIONS

Genius is the transcendent capacity of taking trouble,
first of all.
Thomas Carlyle (1795–1881)

This second project, as the first one in this chapter, is also
complex. However, if you follow the guidelines in the last
section on design considerations you will find that your
embroidering activity will not only be trouble free but also
provide an enjoyable start towards achieving your highest
aspirations.

MATERIALS

Aida, 14 count, 36 x 30 cm (14¼ x 11¾ in)
Tapestry needle, size 24
Roller (or 'tapestry') frame, wider than the fabric width
Strong sewing thread
Tray (available from needlework suppliers)

Threads									
Sranded Cottons	**DMC**	**Anchor**	**Madeira**	**Skeins**	**Sranded Cottons**	**DMC**	**Anchor**	**Madeira**	**Skeins**
White	Blanc	2	2402	2	Off White	746	275	0101	1
Grey Blue dark	926	850	1707	3	Blue ultra very light	3756	1037	1001	1
Grey Blue medium	927	849	1708	1	Grey Blue very light	928	274	1708	1
Grey Blue very dark	3768	779	1106	1	Yellow very light	745	300	0111	1
Grey Blue ultra very dark	924	851	1706	1	Burnt Orange very light	744	301	0112	1

SI SAWAT, THE KORAT

METHOD

1. Prepare the aida and dress the frame as you would for a square or rectangular shaped embroidery (see pages 14–16). Mark the edges of the oval design with tacking stitches as well as the vertical and horizontal central lines.

2. Embroider in full cross stitch.

3. When you have finished the embroidery, remove it from the frame and press it as necessary. Trim the excess fabric leaving enough to fit the inner dimensions of the tray's rectangular shape. Instructions for fitting the embroidery into the tray will be provided by the supplier. The tray illustrated here is from Framecraft (see List of Suppliers, page 143).

KEY

for tray

White
Grey Blue medium
Grey Blue dark
Yellow very light
Grey Blue very light
Grey Blue very dark
Blue ultra very light
Grey Blue ultra very light
Off White
Burnt Orange very light

Stitch count: 125 X 100

KEY

for tray

- · White
- ✦ Grey Blue dark
- Z Grey Blue medium
- ➤ Grey Blue very dark
- ◖ Grey Blue ultra very dark
- ▪ Off White
- ‹ Blue Ultra very light
- ⊠ Grey Blue very light
- — Yellow very light
- ∶ Burnt Orange very light

Stitch count: 125 x 100

KEY

for main project

- White
- Antique Blue very light
- Antique Blue light
- Yellow Ultra very light
- Grey green very light
- Steel Grey light
- Pearl Grey very light
- Antique Blue medium
- Tan very light
- Yellow light

Stitch count: 197 x 147

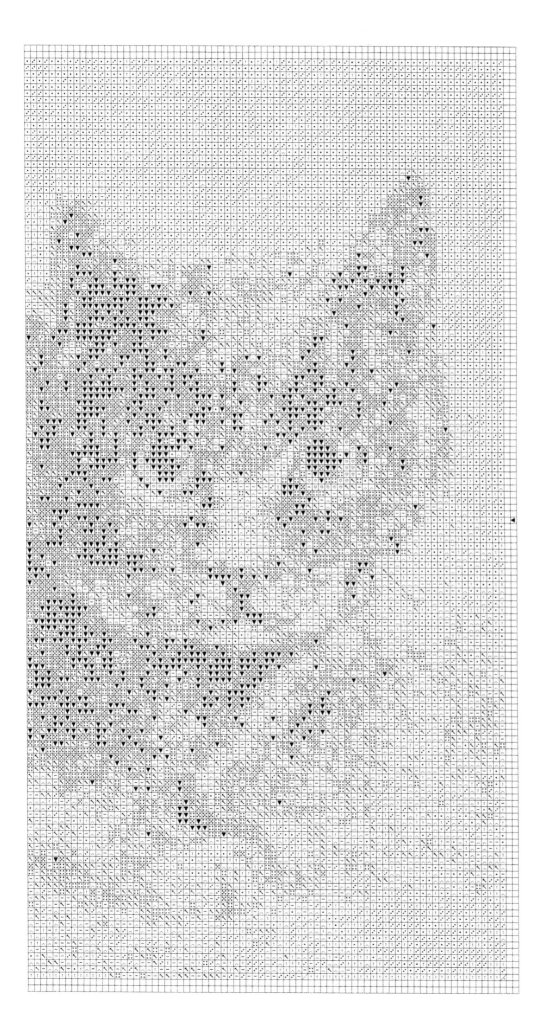

CHAPTER 7

TAFFETA, THE BROWN TABBY **

Size: 33.5 x 27 cm (13¼ x 10½ in)
Embroidered by Liz Phillips

(She) … Draws and dips her body to heap
Her sleepy nerves in a great arm-chair,
Lies defeated and buried deep
Three or four hours unconscious there.
From *Milk for the Cat* by Harold Monro (1879–1932)

The word 'tabby' has a number of possible origins. One may be that it derives from Attibiya, a district in Baghdad where a kind of taffeta, or ribbed silk was made. Another explanation, but linked to the former, is that the word is of Turkish origin deriving from 'utabi', which is the method of calendering, or what is now called 'watering' silk. In the past 'utabi' or 'tabby' used to refer to the fabric itself. The wavy lines on this fabric were so similar to the marking on the fur of certain cats that they became known as 'tabbies'.

DESIGN CONSIDERATIONS

Think of the musical role which colour will
henceforth play …
Colour, which vibrates just like music, is able to
attain what is most general and yet most elusive
in nature – namely its inner force.
Paul Gauguin (1848–1903)

There are two complementary inner forces in this composition. Taffeta is happily resting in her nest of soft green material. At the same time she is strong, alert and possibly unstable as she may jump away at any moment, as cats do. Wassily Kandinsky described green as 'alive but most restful' and orange as 'spreading and strong' with an unstable aspect like 'the balancing of a tightrope walker.' Thus, these two colours together with other modulating colours are used to convey Taffeta's 'inner force' and create a vibration throughout the composition, 'just like music'.

MATERIALS

Aida, 14 count, 40 x 36 cm (16 x 14¼ in)
Tapestry needle, size 24
Roller (or 'tapestry') frame, wider than the fabric width
Strong sewing thread

Threads				
Sranded Cottons	**DMC**	**Anchor**	**Madeira**	**Skeins**
Sranded Cottons	**DMC**	**Anchor**	**Madeira**	**Skeins**
Blue Green	597	168	1108	4
Golden Brown very light	3827	363	2301	3
Violet dark	552	99	2714	2
Baby Blue medium	334	977	1003	2
Cornflower Blue medium dark	3807	122	2702	2
Old Gold light	676	891	2208	2
Golden Yellow very light	3078	292	0102	1
White Bright	B5200	1	2401	1
Hazelnut Brown dark	420	374	2104	1
Yellow light	744	301	0112	1
Baby Pink very light	818	23	0502	1
Topaz very light	727	293	0110	1
Yellow very light	745	300	0111	1
Topaz light	726	295	0109	1
Off White	746	275	0101	1
Baby Blue very light	775	128	0908	1
Brown grey	3787	(393)	1905	1
Blue medium	826	161	1012	1
Lemon medium	307	289	0103	1
Baby Blue medium light	3755	140	0910	1

METHOD

1. Prepare the aida and dress the frame as you would for a square or rectangular-shaped embroidery (see pages 14–16). Mark the edge of the circular design with tacking stitches as well as the vertical and horizontal central lines.

2. Embroider in full cross stitch.

3. Once completed, lace, mount and frame the embroidery (see pages 18–19). Do this by lacing the embroidery on a square sheet of stiff card or board and selecting a mount with a circular aperture (see page 42).

TAFFETA'S HEAD (HANDBAG MIRROR) **

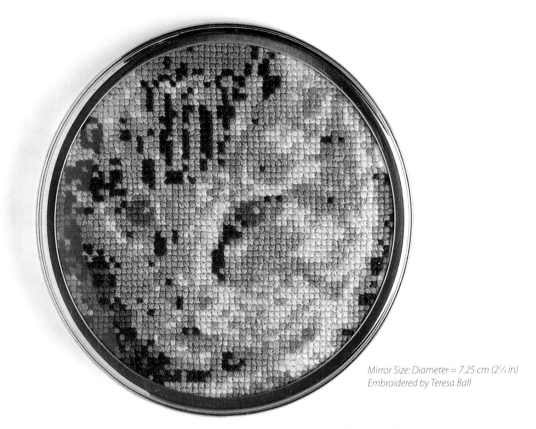

Mirror Size: Diameter = 7.25 cm (2¼ in)
Embroidered by Teresa Ball

Cats are rather delicate creatures and they are subject to a good many ailments,
but I have never heard of one who suffered from insomnia.

Joseph Wood Krutch (1893–1970)

DESIGN CONSIDERATIONS

The simplest patterns are by no means the least beautiful.
From *Art in Needlework* 1900 by Lewis F. Day

The design for this handbag mirror is composed of a similar colour scheme as the main project. However, you will require considerably less threads to embroider it. This is an example of creating a striking and beautiful effect with simplicity.

MATERIALS

Threads				
Sranded Cottons	**DMC**	**Anchor**	**Madeira**	**Skeins**
Golden Brown very light	3827	363	2301	1
Old Gold light	676	891	2208	1
Blue Green	597	168	1108	1
Violet dark	552	99	2714	1
Golden Yellow very light	3078	292	0102	1
Off White	746	285	0101	1
Cornflower Blue				
medium dark	3807	122	2702	1
Baby Pink very light	818	23	0502	1
Baby Blue very light	775	128	0908	1

Evenweave or Aida, 22 count, 15 x 15 cm (6 x 6 in)

Tapestry needle, size 26

Embroidery hoop, 12 cm (5 in) in diameter

Strong sewing thread

Handbag mirror (available from needlework suppliers)

METHOD

1. Prepare the aida and the embroidery hoop (see pages 14–15). Mark out the border and central lines of the design.

2. Embroider in full cross stitch.

3. When you have finished the embroidery, remove it from the embroidery hoop and press it if necessary. Trim the excess fabric leaving a 1 cm (½ in) margin around the edge of the design. Instructions for attaching the embroidery to the mirror will be provided by the supplier. The one illustrated here was supplied by Framecraft (see List of Suppliers, page 143).

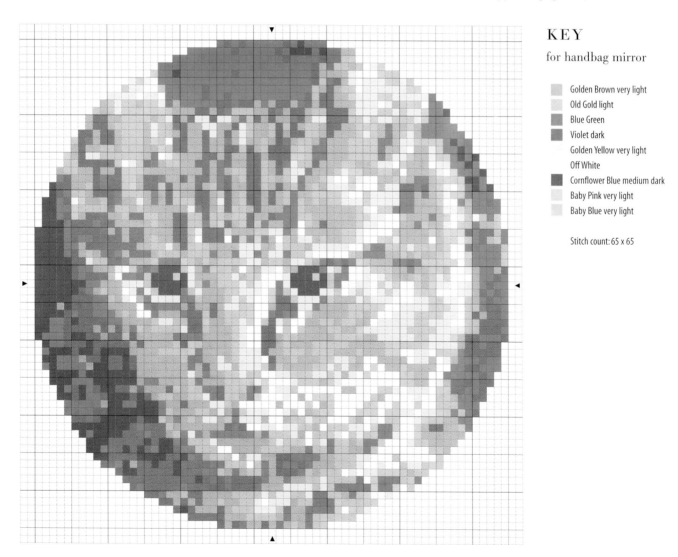

KEY

for handbag mirror

- Golden Brown very light
- Old Gold light
- Blue Green
- Violet dark
- Golden Yellow very light
- Off White
- Cornflower Blue medium dark
- Baby Pink very light
- Baby Blue very light

Stitch count: 65 x 65

TAFFETA, THE BROWN TABBY

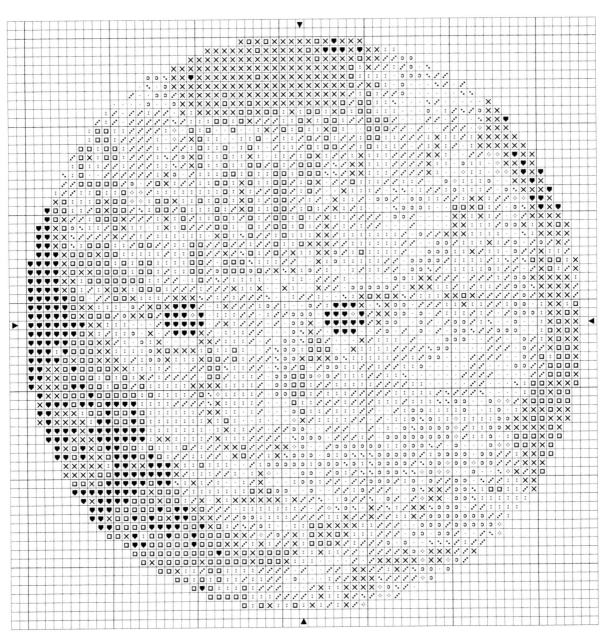

KEY
for handbag mirror

- I   Golden Brown very light
- ▪   Old Gold light
- ✕   Blue Green
- ▢   Violet dark
- ·   Golden Yellow very light
- ◖   Off White
- ♥   Cornflower Blue medium dark
- ▪   Baby Pink very light
- ◇   Baby Blue very light

Stitch count: 65 x 65

KEY
for main project

- Blue Green
- Golden Brown very light
- Violet dark
- Baby Blue medium
- Cornflower Blue medium dark
- Old Gold light
- Golden Yellow very light
- White Bright
- Hazelnut Brown dark
- Yellow light
- Baby Pink very light

- Topaz very light
- Yellow very light
- Topaz light
- Off White
- Baby Blue very light
- Brown grey
- Blue medium
- Lemon medium
- Baby Blue medium light

Stitch count: 188 X 150

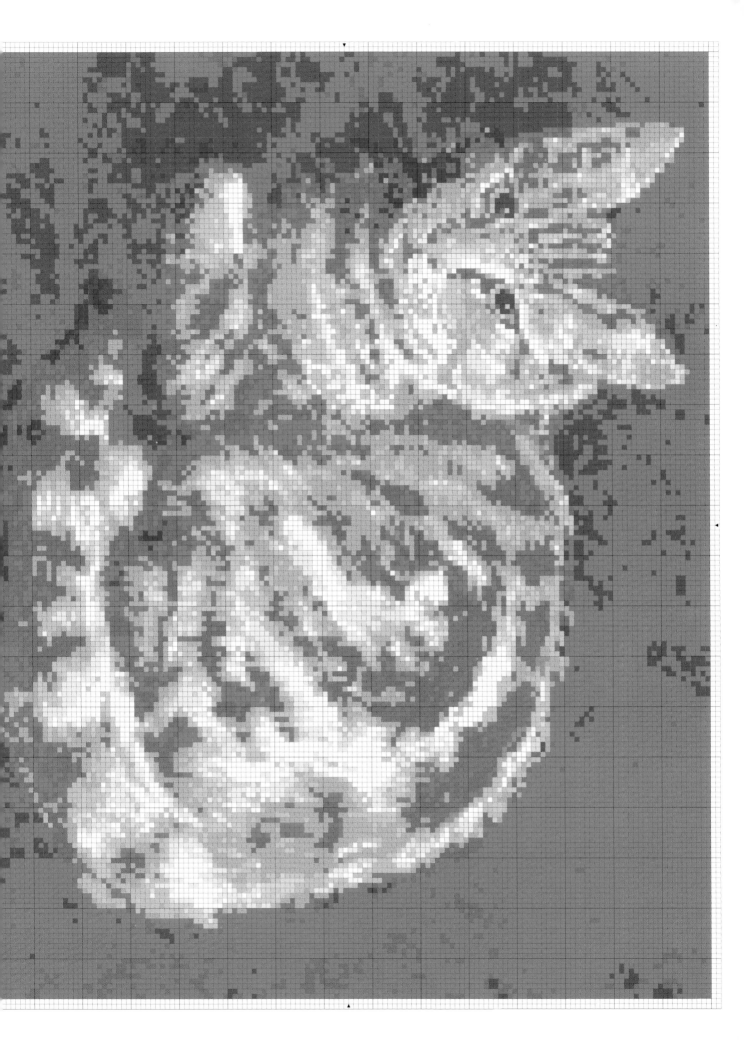

KEY

for main project

- ✳ Blue Green
- I Golden Brown very light
- ⊡ Violet dark
- ⌗ Baby Blue medium
- ♥ Cornflower Blue medium dark
- (Old Gold light
- ! Golden Yellow very light
- · White Bright
- ☐ Hazelnut Brown dark
- ♡ Yellow light
- ∧ Baby Pink very light
- ⫶ Topaz very light
- ∨ Yellow very light
- ⫶ Topaz light
- ⊃ Off White
- ◇ Baby Blue very light
- ● Brown grey
- ▲ Blue medium
- ⊢ Lemon medium
- ▲ Baby Blue medium light

Stitch count: 188 X 150

CHAPTER 8
WILLOW,
THE MOGGIE **

Size: 20.5 x 25.5 cm (8 x 10 in)
Embroidered by Joy Spencer

I like little Pussy, her coat is so warm,

And if I don't hurt her she'll do me no harm;

So I'll not pull her tail, nor drive her away,

But Pussy and I very gently will play.

From I Like Little Pussy (1830), Anonymous

There is a legend that if kittens are thrown into rivers to be drowned they will be rescued by willow trees. As the legend goes, once upon a time the mother cat of such unfortunate kittens wept so bitterly that the willows on the nearby bank felt such compassion that they held out their compliant branches to the struggling kittens and each one of them was saved. Ever since that time, each Spring the willows put out grey buds that feel as soft and silky as the coats of little kittens, thus these trees are now called pussy willows.

DESIGN CONSIDERATIONS

Gradation in colour expresses a series of adroitly managed transitions …
to be employed according to the feelings intended …
From *Needlework as Art* (1886) by Lady Marion M. Alford

One of the many meanings of the word 'design' is intent or the inner purpose of a composition. The intention of this picture of Willow is to create the tender love of a mother cat, as befits the legend. Therefore the tonal values in this project modulate gradually from dark to light in order to express this tenderness. For the same reason the intensity of all the colours are dull and muted. However, in order to prevent the composition from appearing drab and lifeless, most of the pale colours are biased toward orange and all of the greys are biased toward blue. This complementary pair of colours enlivens the effect without disturbing the unity of the composition.

MATERIALS

Aida, 14 Count, 31 x 36 cm (12¼ x 14¼ in)
Tapestry needle, size 24
Roller (or 'tapestry') frame, wider than the fabric width
Strong sewing thread

Threads									
Sranded Cottons	**DMC**	**Anchor**	**Madeira**	**Skeins**	**Sranded Cottons**	**DMC**	**Anchor**	**Madeira**	**Skeins**
Steel Grey light	318	399	1802	2	Antique Violet light	3042	869	2611	1
Antique Violet medium	3041	871	0806	2	Ecru	Ecrut	387	2314	1
Brown Grey very light	3024	397	1901	2	Beige Brown ultra very light	543	933	0306	1
Antique Blue medium	931	1034	1711	2	Antique Violet very light	3743	869	2611	1
Pearl Grey	415	398	1802	2	Green Grey very light	928	274	1708	1
Antique Blue light	932	1033	1710	1	Pearl Grey very light	762	234	1709	1
Mocha Brown light	3033	391	1907	1	Cornflower Blue				
Beige Brown very light	842	376	1910	1	medium dark	3807	122	2702	1
Brown Grey light	3023	(899)	1906	1					

METHOD

1. Prepare the aida and dress the frame as you would for a square- or rectangular-shaped embroidery (see pages 14–16). Mark the edges of the oval design with tacking stitches as well as the vertical and horizontal central lines.

2. Embroider in full cross stitch.

3. Once completed, lace, mount and frame the embroidery. Do this by lacing the embroidery on a square sheet of stiff card or board and selecting a mount with an oval aperture (see page 42).

WILLOW'S FACE (ELM BOX LID) **

Size: 7.5 x 8.5 cm (3 x 3¼ in)
Embroidered by Elizabeth Hadwick

The cat is the only animal that accepts the comforts but
rejects the bondage of domesticity.
Georges Louis Leclerc de Buffon (1707–1788)

DESIGN CONSIDERATIONS

Actually, you work with only a few colours. But they seem a lot more when you put them in the right place.

Pablo Picasso (1881–1973)

The number of colours for the design for the Elm Box Lid are considerably less than those for the main project in this chapter. Willow's characteristics are love and tender affection. By choosing only a few colours and putting them in the right place, these qualities are conveyed; as Thomas a Kempis said, 'Simplicity is in the intention, purity in the affection.'

MATERIALS

Threads				
Sranded Cottons	**DMC**	**Anchor**	**Madeira**	**Skeins**
Antique Blue light	932	1033	1710	1
Beige Brown very light	842	376	1910	1
Antique Blue medium	931	1034	1711	1
Antique Violet medium	3041	871	0806	1
Mocha Brown light	3033	391	1907	1
Ecru	Ecrut	387	2314	1
Pearl Grey	415	398	1802	1
Cornflower Blue				
medium dark	3807	122	2702	1
Grey Green very light	928	274	1708	1

Aida, 16 count, 15 x 15 cm (6 x 6 in)

Tapestry needle, size 24

Embroidery hoop, 12 cm (5 in) in diameter

Strong sewing thread

Elm box (available from needlecraft suppliers)

METHOD

1. Prepare the aida and the embroidery hoop (see pages 14–15). Mark out the border and central lines of the design.

2. Embroider in full cross stitch.

3. When you have finished the embroidery, remove it from the embroidery hoop and press it if necessary. Trim the excess fabric leaving a 1 cm (½ in) margin around the edge of the design. Instructions for fitting the embroidery into the lid of the box will be provided by the supplier. The one illustrated here is from Framecraft (see List of Suppliers, page 143).

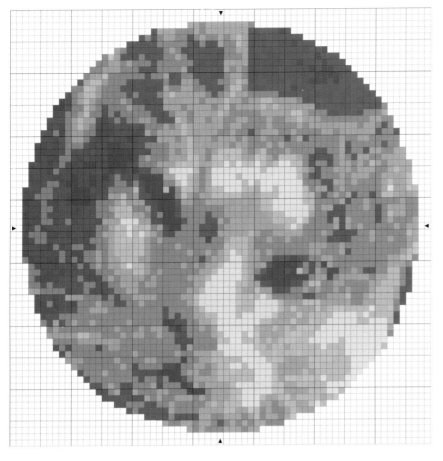

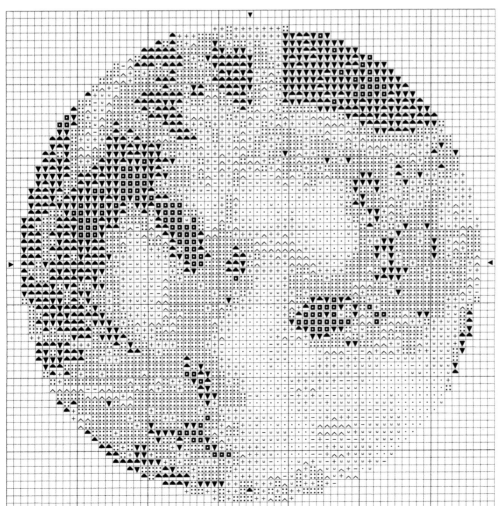

KEY

for main project

- :: Steel Grey light
- ▲ Antique Violet medium
- ╱ Brown Grey medium
- ▼ Antique Blue medium
- ∧ Pearl Grey
- :: Antique Blue light
- ω Mocha Brown light
- + Beige Brown very light
- ✦ Brown Grey light
- S Antique Violet light
- — Green Grey very light
- ɔ Antique Violet very light
- · Beige Brown ultra very light
- I Ecru
- ∧ Pearl Grey very light
- ◼ Cornflower Blue medium dark

Stitch count: 113 X 163

CHAPTER 9
SINH, THE BIRMAN ***

Size: Diameter = 34 cm (13½ in)
Embroidered by Ruth Fitzgerald

*To gain the friendship of a cat is a difficult thing. The cat is
a philosophical, methodical, quiet animal, tenacious of its own
habits, fond of order and cleanliness, and it does not lightly
confer its friendship… But if he once gives himself to you it is with
absolute confidence and affection!*
From *La Menagerie Intime* (1850) by Theophile Gautier (1811–1872)

In Ancient Burma it was believed that white long-haired cats with yellow eyes guarded the temple dedicated to the golden, blue eyed goddess Tsun-Kyan-Kse. One day the high priest was mortally wounded by cruel invaders. His favourite cat, whose name was Sinh, leapt onto the body of his master. Looking up into the sapphire blue eyes of the goddess Sinh comforted his master until he died. At once the soul of the priest entered the cat whose fur turned gold and whose eyes became sapphire blue. His nose, ears, legs and tail darkened to take on the colour of the earth but his paws, still resting on the body of his master, remained white as a symbol of purity. This is how the sacred cat of Burma came into being, and why the cat in this project is called Sinh.

DESIGN CONSIDERATIONS

It is not because things are difficult that we do not dare; it is because we do not dare that they are difficult.'
Seneca (circa 3BC–AD65)

This is a complex design, but avoid allowing any negative thoughts and imagined difficulties to enter your mind. If they do, remember that difficulties, as such, reside in the mind and only in the mind. They can be dismissed as quickly as they are allowed to enter. If you 'dare' to embroider this main project of Sinh, the Birman, read again the Design Considerations for the main project in Chapter

Six on page 61, which discuss design strategies and ways in which you may journey through your embroidering adventure serenely, efficiently and contentedly.

After you have dared to start embroidering, you will soon discover a warm golden glow emanating from the representation of Sinh and his surroundings. This is because orange, yellow and warm brown colours predominate and are enhanced and complemented by small amounts of grey biased towards blue. All such artifices have been contrived to convey the moment of Sinh's fur turning gold, as described in the legend.

MATERIALS

Threads

Sranded Cottons	DMC	Anchor	Madeira	Skeins	Sranded Cottons	DMC	Anchor	Madeira	Skeins
White Bright	B5200	1	2401	3	Antique Mauve light	3726	1018	0810	1
Beige Brown light	841	378	2601	3	Pearly Grey very light	762	234	1709	1
Brown Grey light	3023	(899)	1906	3	Tan medium light	437	362	2012	1
Drab Brown light	613	831	2109	2	Flesh light	950	4146	2309	1
Antique Mauve medium	316	1017	0809	2	Khaki Green light	3013	842	1605	1
Mocha Brown medium dark	3032	903	2002	1	Brown Grey medium	3022	8581	1812	1
Antique Violet medium	3041	871	0806	1	Beige Brown dark	839	(360)	2005	1
Avocado medium	371	854	2110	1	Salmon very light	3713	1020	0808	1
Beige Grey medium	644	830	2001	1	Peach Flesh very light	948	1011	2308	1
Antique Violet light	3042	870	0807	1	Flesh medium	3773	1008	2312	1
Yellow Beige light	3047	852	2109	1	Antique Blue very light	3752	1032	0908	1
Beige Brown very light	842	376	1901	1	Golden Yellow very light	3078	292	0102	1
Shell Grey dark	451	233	1808	1	Hazelnut Brown medium	3828	943	2102	1
Pewter Grey	317	400	1714	1	Pewter Grey dark	413	401	1713	1

SINH, THE BIRMAN

Aida, 14 count, 48 x 48 cm (19 x 19 in)

Tapestry needle, size 24

Roller (or 'tapestry') frame, wider than the fabric width

Strong sewing thread

METHOD

1. Prepare the aida and dress the frame as you would for a square or rectangular shaped embroidery (see pages 14–16). Mark the edge of the circular design with tacking stitches as well as the vertical and horizontal central lines.

2. Embroider in full cross stitch.

3. Once completed, lace, mount and frame the embroidery. Do this by lacing the embroidery on a square sheet of stiff card or board and selecting a mount with a circular aperture (see pages 18–19).

SINH'S HEAD (TABLE TOP) **

Nothing is more playful than a young cat, nor more grave than an old one.

Thomas Fuller (1608–1661)

Size: Diameter = 29 cm (11½ in)
Embroidered by Sue Fielding

DESIGN CONSIDERATIONS

Gold is a wonderful clearer of understanding … It silences the loud and clamorous, and brings over the most obstinate and inflexible.

Joseph Addison (1672–1719)

There are fewer colours in this second project than those used in the main project. Nevertheless, oranges, yellows and warm browns predominate still, and are augmented by the cool, complementary bluish-greys. All are intended to create the illusion of gold. Cat connoisseurs will instantly recognise that I have taken artistic liberties, because such colours are only present in the body fur of this cat and not in the head. 'Exactitude is not the truth,' said Matisse, and Paul Klee said, 'art does not reproduce the visible but makes visible.' Therefore, I believe I have the sanction to 'lie' in order to realize the 'truth' about the legend of Sinh.

MATERIALS

Aida, 14 count, 50 x 50 cm (20 x 20 in)
Tapestry needle, size 24
Roller (or 'tapestry') frame, wider than the fabric width
Strong sewing thread

METHOD

1. Prepare the aida and dress the frame as you would for a square or rectangular shaped embroidery (see pages 14–16). Mark the edge of the circular design with tacking stitches as well as the vertical and horizontal central lines.

2. Embroider in full cross stitch.

PLACING THE EMBROIDERY ONTO THE TABLE TOP

Materials

The finished embroidery
A table whose top is circular, of which the inner diameter is 29 cm (11½ in)
A circular sheet of glass with the same dimensions as the table top
A circular sheet of stiff card or laminated board whose diameter is 28 cm (11¼ in)
Strong sewing thread

Method

1. Remove the embroidery from the frame and press it if necessary. Trim the fabric leaving 1cm (½ in) margin around the embroidery.

2. Lay the embroidery face downwards onto a clean surface. Place the card or board onto the back of the embroidery. Stitch around the margin with running stitch. Gently pull the thread so that the margin of the fabric turns round the edge of the board. Ensure that the embroidery is centralized.

3. Place the embroidery onto the table top and cover with the glass.

Threads									
Sranded Cottons	DMC	Anchor	Madeira	Skeins	Sranded Cottons	DMC	Anchor	Madeira	Skeins
Antique Violet medium	3041	871	0806	2	Pearl Grey very light	762	234	1709	1
Brown Grey medium	3022	8581	1812	2	Pewter Grey	317	400	1714	1
Khaki Green light	3013	842	1605	2	Tan medium light	437	362	2012	1
Brown Grey light	3023	(899)	1906	2	Flesh medium	3773	1008	2312	1
Antique Violet light	3042	870	0807	2	Antique Mauve medium	316	1017	0809	1
Flesh light	950	4146	2309	2	Antique Blue very light	3752	1032	0908	1
Golden Yellow very light	3078	292	0102	1	Pewter Grey dark	413	401	1713	1
Peach Flesh very light	948	1011	2308	1					

KEYS

for table top

 Antique Violet medium	Pewter Grey
Brown Grey medium	Tan medium light
Khaki Green light	Flesh medium
Brown Grey light	Antique Mauve medium
Antique Violet light	Antique Blue very light
Flesh light	Pewter Grey dark
Golden Yellow very light	
Peach Flesh very light	Stitch count: 107 x 107
Pearl Grey very light	

 ✄ Antique Violet medium	▫ Pewter Grey
⊟ Brown Grey medium	⚒ Tan medium light
Ɛ Khaki Green light	∩ Flesh medium
✦ Brown Grey light	Antique Mauve medium
◪ Antique Violet light	↖ Antique Blue very light
∿ Flesh light	● Pewter Grey dark
· Golden Yellow very light	
Ɔ Peach Flesh very light	Stitch count: 107 x 107
∧ Pearl Grey very light	

KEY

for main project

- Beige Brown light
- Brown Grey light
- Drab Brown light
- Antique Mauve medium
- White Bright
- Mocha Brown medium dark
- Antique Violet medium
- Avocado medium
- Beige Grey medium
- Antique Violet light
- Yellow Beige light
- Beige Brown very light
- Shell Grey dark
- Pewter Grey
- Antique Mauve light
- Pearl Grey very light
- Tan medium light
- Flesh light
- Khaki Green light
- Brown Grey medium
- Beige Brown dark
- Salmon very light
- Peach Flesh very light
- Flesh medium
- Antique Blue very light
- Golden Yellow light
- Hazelnut Brown medium
- Pewter Grey dark

Stitch count: 189 X 192

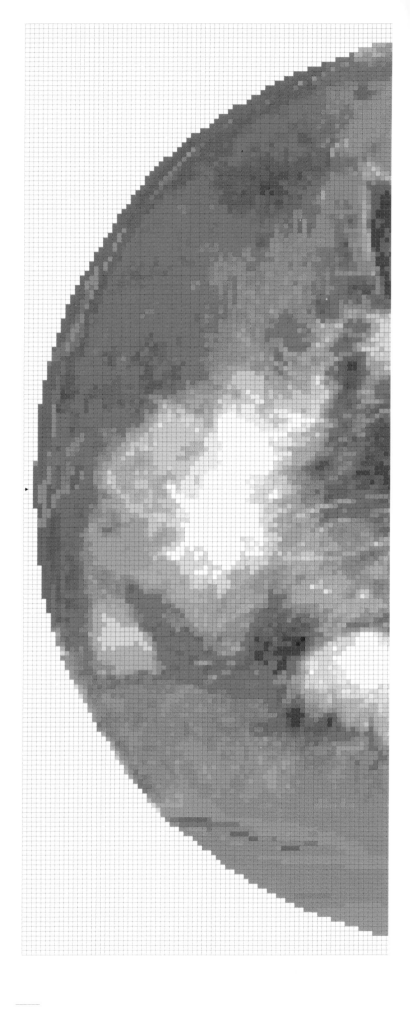

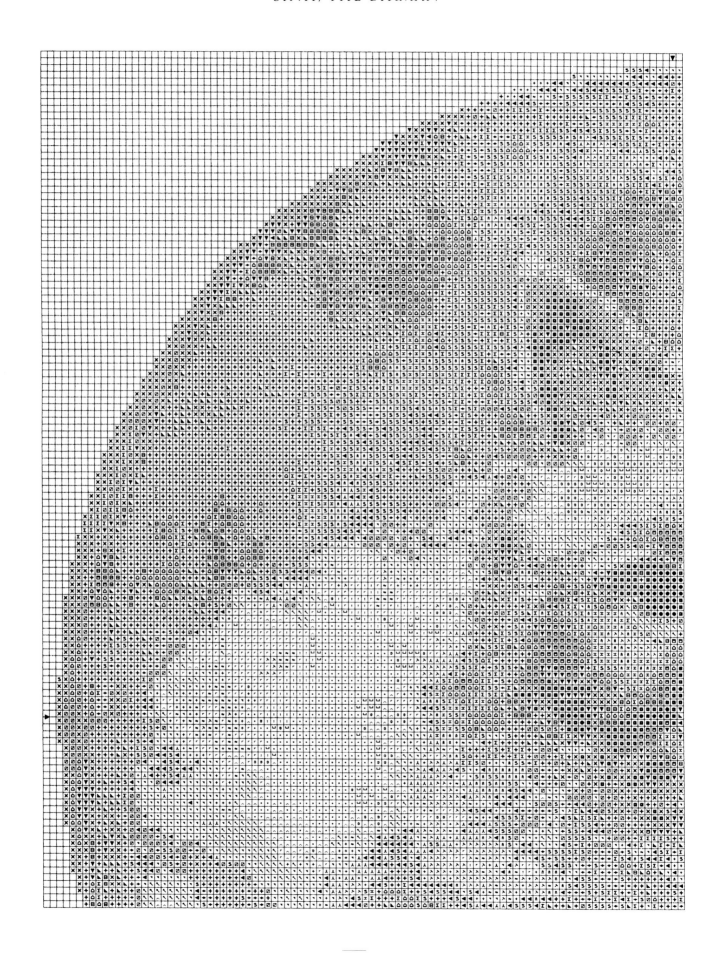

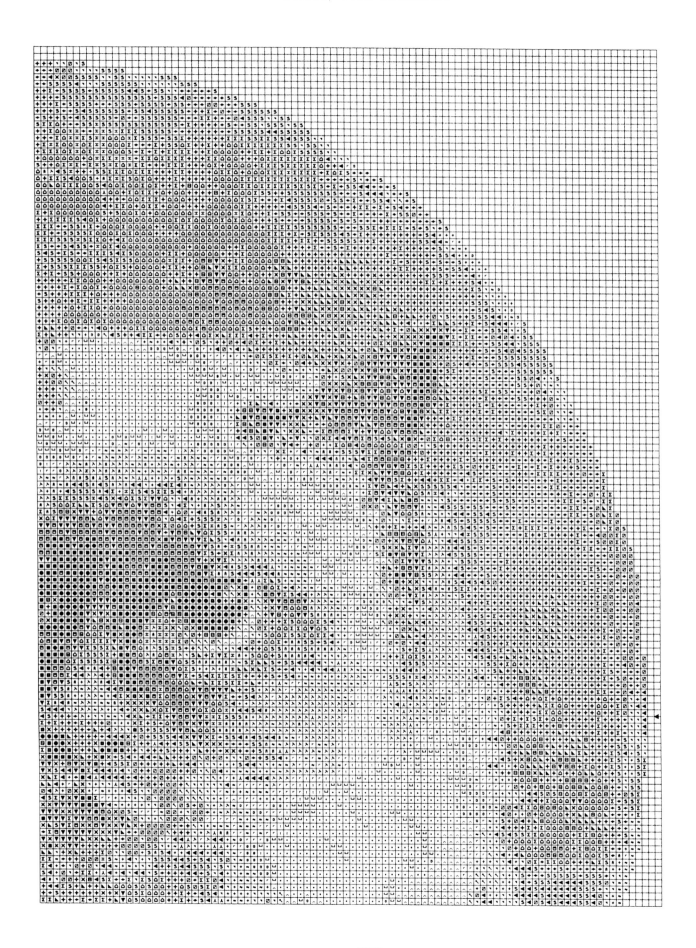

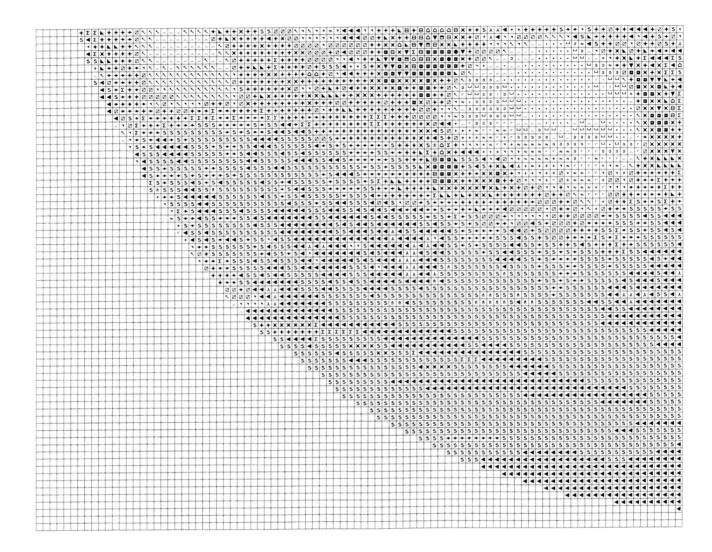

KEY

for main project

S	White Bright		∧	Pearly Grey very light
✦	Beige Brown light		⋊	Tan medium light
◀	Brown Grey light		∾	Flesh light
◆	Drab Brown light		人	Khaki Green light
·	Antique Mauve medium		⊟	Brown Grey medium
Σ	Mocha Brown medium dark		▭	Beige Brown dark
✕	Antique Violet medium		ᴐ	Salmon very light
△	Avocado medium		⊔	Peach Flesh very light
◣	Beige Grey medium		∩	Flesh medium
⧄	Antique Violet light		↖	Antique Blue very light
┌	Yellow Beige light		!	Golden Yellow very light
+	Beige Brown very light		⊥	Hazelnut Brown medium
◤	Shell Grey dark		●	Pewter Grey dark
◘	Pewter Grey			
▼	Antique Mauve light			

Stitch count: 189 X 192

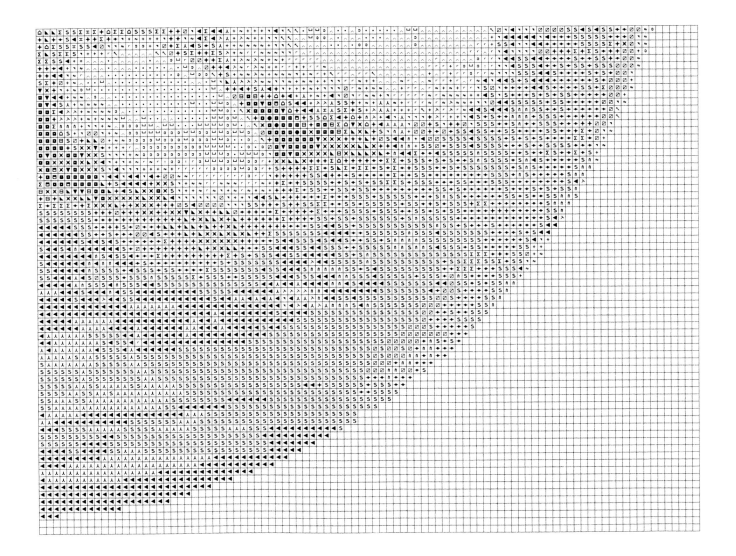

CHAPTER 10
GINGER, THE KITTEN ***

Size: 29 x 40.5 cm (11½ x 6 in)
Embroidered by Marcia Gooder

Always it's pouncing at nothing

Striking with both paws at once.

Although there is nothing to see

It seems that the kitten sees something.

From *The Kitten* by W.W.E. Ross (1894–1966)

This ginger kitten looks very lost and shy. However, do not let him beguile you. He is a relation of the red tabby and, like the spice, he can be a little fiery at times, befitting his name. In fact, he is probably on the point of 'pouncing at nothing' at any minute. Ginger typically carries an 'M' on his forehead in true tabby style. According to legend, this mark was created by the prophet Mohammed when he rested his hand gently on the brow of his favourite cat.

DESIGN CONSIDERATIONS

Rules are part of the game, they are not outside it.
No rules; then no game.
Different rules: then a different game.
From *Experience and Education* (1931) by John Dewey

This design shows how the rules about juxtaposing complementary colours can be adapted to suit the nature of the subject. In this case, I wanted to portray Ginger as a conspicuously fiery kitten. Therefore the complementary colour of the background blue is a deliberate rival to the orange which constitutes much of Ginger's construction. Nevertheless, I have used three devices to tone down the effect of this contrast. Firstly, whereas the bright orange colours remain bright, the majority of blues are dull, dark and almost grey. Secondly, all the blues which constitute the background are to be found in less quantity in the shadows of Ginger's fiery fur in order to unify the composition. Thirdly, there are three specific colours present in the composition of Ginger's fur, which are almost imperceptible until you start to embroider this project. These colours are 'rose' (pink) 'green' and 'sky blue'. In his book *Della Pittura* of 1435, Leon Battista Alberti wrote 'Rose near green and sky blue give honour and life.' Thus even though they are only present in small quantities, these three colours exercise an honorably disciplined role in the composition, relating both to harmony and intention.

MATERIALS

Threads									
Sranded Cottons	**DMC**	**Anchor**	**Madeira**	**Skeins**	**Sranded Cottons**	**DMC**	**Anchor**	**Madeira**	**Skeins**
Grey Green Medium	926	850	1707	3	Cream	712	926	1908	1
Delft medium	799	136	0910	2	Antique Mauve medium	316	1017	0809	1
Yellow very light	745	300	0111	2	Golden Brown very light	3827	363	2301	1
Baby Blue light	3325	129	0907	1	Flesh light	950	4146	2309	1
Pearl Grey	415	398	1802	1	Yellow Beige light	3047	852	2109	1
Hazelnut Brown medium	3828	943	2102	1	Mahogany very light	402	1047	2307	1
Tan Medium light	437	362	2012	1	Avocado Green pale	472	(253)	1604	1
Topaz very light	727	293	0110	1	White Bright	B5200	1	2401	1
Laurel Green dark	3363	262	1602	1	Tangerine light	742	303	0114	1
Khaki Green light	3013	842	1605	1	Avocado Green very light	471	266	1502	1
Gold very light	834	874	2510	1	Melon light	3708	31	0408	1
Salmon very light	3713	1020	0808	1					

Aida, 14 count, 40 x 50 cm (16 x 20 in)
Tapestry needle, size 24
Roller (or 'tapestry') frame, wider than the fabric width
Strong sewing thread

GINGER, THE KITTEN

METHOD

1. Prepare the aida and dress the frame (see pages 14–16). Mark out the central lines of the design.

2. Embroider in full cross stitch.

3. Once completed, lace, mount and frame the embroidery (see pages 18–19).

Dilated swells thy glossy fur
And loudly croons thy busy purr
As timing well the equal sound
Thy clutching feet bepat the ground.
From *The Kitten* by Joanna Baille (1762–1851)

GINGER'S FACE (LARGE COASTER) **

No matter how much cats fight,
there always seem to be plenty of kittens.
Abraham Lincoln 1809–1865

DESIGN CONSIDERATIONS

This is not a technique for those who want to finish a piece of work quickly. The fascination lies in the leisurely in-and-out motion of the needle (and its little sound) and the thoughtful contemplation of its colourful design.
Helena Baily (1910–1996)

If we take advice from the wisest and most experienced of our embroidering friends such as Helena Baily, we shall learn that the way we organise and 'design' ourselves is important. Quite clearly the application of three of the senses – listening, touching and watching – will develop our powers of focused attention. Not only will our embroidering skills become more efficient, but also the process will become more enjoyable.

Size: Diameter = 9 cm (3 ½ in)
Embroidered by Kitty Mogford

MATERIALS

Threads				
Sranded Cottons	DMC	Anchor	Madeira	Skeins
Laurel Green dark	3363	262	1602	1
Hazelnut Brown medium	3828	943	2102	1
Tan medium light	437	362	2012	1
Gold very light	834	874	2510	1
Pearl Grey	415	398	1802	1
Salmon very light	3713	1020	0808	1
Yellow very light	745	300	0111	1
Mahogany very light	402	1047	2307	1

Aida, 14 count, 15 x 15 cm (6 x 6 in)

Tapestry needle, size 14

Embroidery hoop, 12 cm (5 in) in diameter

Strong sewing thread

Large coaster (available from needlework suppliers)

METHOD

1. Prepare the aida and the embroidery hoop (see pages 14–15). Mark out the borders and central lines on the designs.

2. Embroider in full cross stitch.

3. When you have finished the embroidery, remove it from the embroidery hoop and press it if necessary. Trim the excess fabric leaving a 1 cm (½ in) margin around the edges of the design. Instructions for fitting the embroidery into the coaster will be provided by the supplier. The one illustrated here is from Framecraft (see List of Suppliers, page 143).

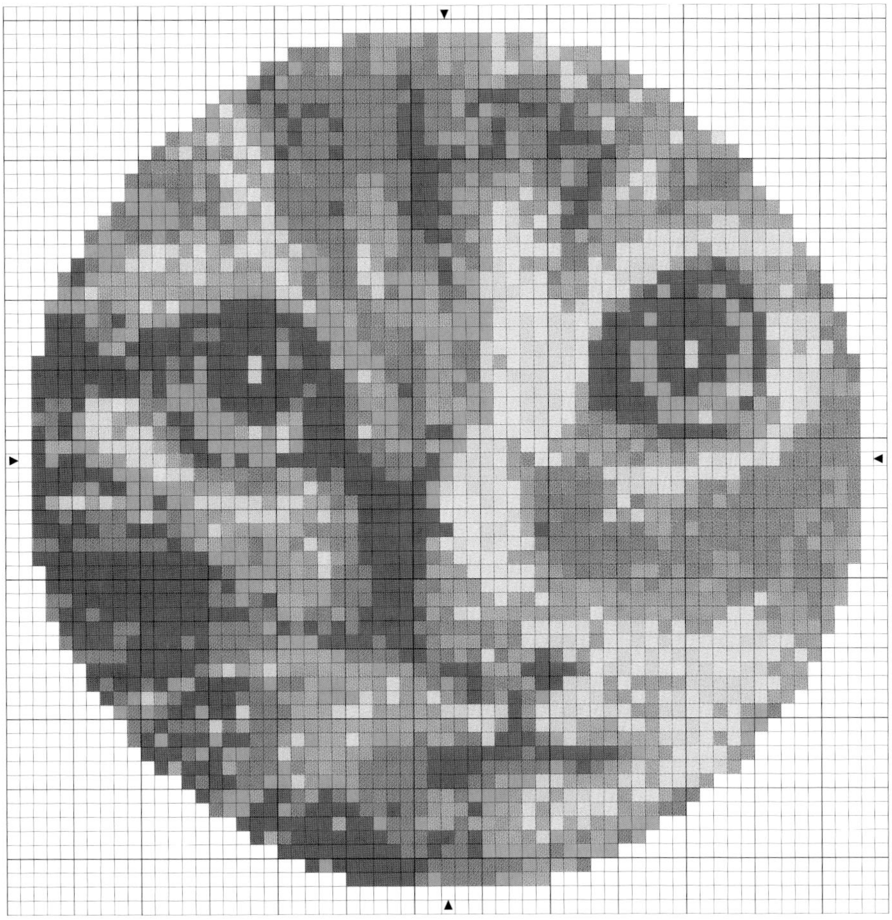

KEY

for main project

(those also used for coaster are indicated with an asterisk)

- Grey Green Medium
- Delft medium
- Yellow very light*
- Baby Blue light
- Pearl Grey*
- Hazelnut Brown medium*
- Tan Medium light*
- Topaz very light
- Laurel Green dark*
- Khaki Green light
- Gold very light*
- Salmon very light*
- Cream
- Antique Mauve medium
- Golden Brown very light
- Flesh light
- Yellow Beige light
- Mahogany very light*
- Avocado Green pale
- White Bright
- Tangerine light
- Avocado Green very light
- Melon light

Stitch count: 61 x 61 (coaster)
159 x 225 (main project)

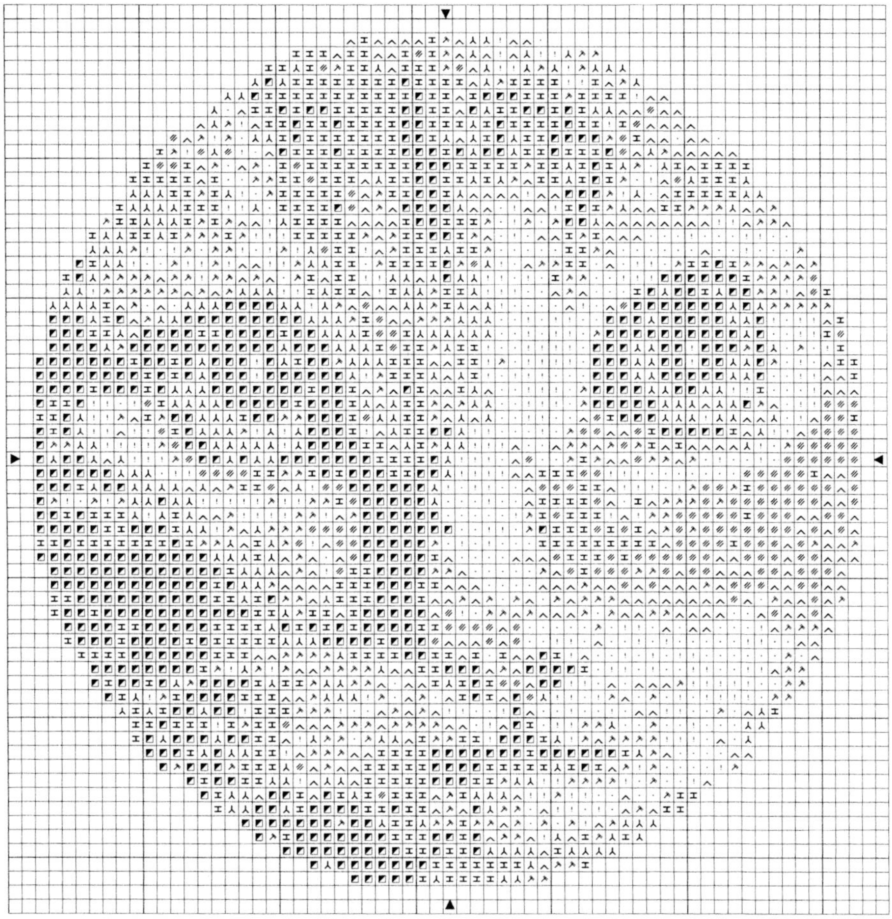

KEY

for coaster

- Laurel Green dark
- Hazelnut Brown medium
- Gold very light
- Pearl Grey
- Tan medium light
- Yellow very light
- Salmon very light
- Mahogany very light

Stitch count: 61 x 61

KEY

for main project

- ☐ Grey Green Medium
- Ⅱ Delft medium
- ▪ Yellow very light
- ✦ Baby Blue light
- ᐸ Pearl Grey
- Ⅱ Hazelnut Brown medium
- ⟋ Tan Medium light
- : Topaz very light
- ◪ Laurel Green dark
- 人 Khaki Green light
- ⋀ Gold very light
- 2 Salmon very light
- 1 Cream
- ⬚ Antique Mauve medium
- ⩘ Golden Brown very light
- ∿ Flesh light
- ᴦ Yellow Beige light
- ⫽ Mahogany very light
- ᴩ Avocado Green pale
- • White Bright
- c Tangerine light
- ⋂ Avocado Green very light
- ꞁ Melon light

Stitch count:159 X 225

CHAPTER 11

MAU, THE TABBY KITTEN ***

Size: 26 x 31 cm (10¼ x 12¼ in)
Embroidered by Rob Halbert

The male cat is Ra himself, and he was called Mau because
of the speech of the god Sa, who said concerning him:
'He is like unto that which he hath made,
therefore, did the name of Ra become Mau.

Written on a fragment of papyrus from Ancient Egypt (circa 1500 BC)

This kitten is called Mau because he looks as if he is saying 'miauw' or 'mau'. It is always important to talk to our cats and kittens – although they will not understand the meaning of our words, they will appreciate the sound of our voices, just as we appreciate theirs.

DESIGN CONSIDERATIONS

True beauty results from that repose which the mind feels when the eye, the intellect, and the affections, are satisfied from the absence of any want.
From *The Grammar of Ornament* (1856) by Owen Jones.

Pale tones of dull blues and greys complement similar tones of dull orange to express the gentle yet lively quality of this tabby kitten. Very pale, dull yellows contrasting with dark, muted mauves and violet manifest his form and contribute to his liveliness. This, together with the gradation of tones between the subject and his background are all intended to create beauty in the composition. Furthermore, when you embroider this project you should feel a sense of repose in your mind as the composition forms before your eyes.

MATERIALS

Aida, 14 count, 36 x 41 cm (14¼ x 16 in)
Tapestry needle, size 24
Roller (or 'tapestry') frame, whose width is wider than the fabric
Strong sewing thread

METHOD

1. Prepare the aida, dress the frame (see pages 14–16) and mark out the border and central lines of the design.

2. Embroider in full cross stitch.

3. Once completed, frame, mount and lace the embroidery (see pages 18–19).

Note: This design is complex and therefore probably best attempted once you have gained experience in embroidering. It involves concentrating on distinguishing a number of subtle colours. When embroidering, you will need to work in a clear light.

Threads									
Sranded Cottons	**DMC**	**Anchor**	**Madeira**	**Skeins**	**Sranded Cottons**	**DMC**	**Anchor**	**Madeira**	**Skeins**
White	Blanc	2	2402	1	Steel Grey light	318	399	1802	1
Antique Violet very light	3743	869	2611	2	Brown Grey very light	3024	397	1901	1
Pearl Grey	415	398	1802	2	Beige Brown very light	842	376	1910	1
Mocha Brown light	3033	391	1907	2	Antique Blue very light	3752	1032	0908	1
Antique Violet light	3042	870	0807	2	Shell Grey medium	452	232	1807	1
Pearl Grey very light	762	234	1709	2	Antique Blue ultra very light	3753	1031	1001	1
Off White	746	275	0101	1	Brown Grey light	3023	(899)	1906	1
Beige Grey medium	644	830	2001	1	Salmon very light	3713	1020	0808	1
Ecru	Ecrut	387	2314	1	Antique Violet medium	3041	871	0806	1
Antique Blue light	932	1033	1710	1	Antique Mauve medium	316	1017	0809	1
Grey Green very light	928	274	1708	1	Sportsman Flesh light	951	1010	2308	1
Beaver Grey very light	3072	(847)	1805	1					

MAU'S HEAD (HERB PILLOW) **

*The playful kitten with its little tigerish gambole is infinitely
more amusing than half the people one is obliged to live with
in the world.*

Lady Sidney Morgan (1783–1859)

DESIGN CONSIDERATIONS

*To decorate or ornament an object is to enrich the surface
with forms and colour, and thus to give the thing decorated a
new beauty while adhering strictly to its original shape and
character.*

From *Embroidery or the Craft of the Needle* (1907) by
W.G. Paulson Townsend

Similar hues and tones of colours which are used for the
main project in this chapter are used again here for the herb
pillow but in fewer numbers. This array of colours seems
eminently suitable to convey Mau's sweet and gentle nature.
Moreover, the colours also 'adhere' to the 'character' of this
decorated object whose shape and purpose is to comfort us
and develop the sweet and gentle natures in us.

Size: Diameter = 12 cm (4 3/4 in)
Embroidered by Sue Fielding

MATERIALS

Threads				
Sranded Cottons	**DMC**	**Anchor**	**Madeira**	**Skeins**
Antique Blue very light	3752	1032	0908	1
Antique Violet very light	3743	869	2611	1
Antique Blue light	932	1033	1710	1
Mocha Brown light	3033	391	1907	1
Cream	712	926	1908	1
Beige Grey medium	644	830	2001	1
Steel Grey light	318	399	1802	1
Shell Grey medium	452	232	1807	1

Aida, 14 count, 24 x 24 cm (9½ x 9½ in)

Tapestry needle, size 24

Embroidery hoop or rectangular stretcher frame,
    20 x 20 cm (8 x 8 in)

Strong sewing thread

METHOD

1. Prepare the aida and the hoop, or stretcher frame (see
    pages 14–15). Mark out the border and central lines.

2. Embroider in full cross stitch.

3. When you have finished the embroidery, follow the next
    set of instructions to make the Herb Pillow.

MAKING THE HERB PILLOW
Materials
The completed embroidery of Mau's Head

A square of white cotton fabric, 20 x 20 cm (8 x 8 in)

One metre of cord

Soft padding

Sweet herbs such as thyme and rosemary, or even lavender,
   dried and stitched into a small muslin bag

Method
1. Remove the embroidery from the frame and press it if
   necessary. Place it face upwards onto a clean surface.
   Trim excess fabric so that a margin of about 1 cm (½ in)
   remains around the outer raw edges of the fabric.

2. Lay the square of white cotton fabric onto the face of the
embroidery and secure with the pins already used for the
edging. Stitch through the two layers all round and up to
the edge of the embroidery, but leave a gap of about
5 cm (2 in) at one edge.

3. Remove all pins, turn inside out and insert the soft
padding and muslin bag in the now formed cushion cover.
Close the gap by stitching it. Finish by sewing the cord
around all four edges.

KEY

for main project

White
Antique Violet very light
Pearl Grey
Mocha Brown light
Antique Violet light
Pearl Grey very light
Off White
Beige Grey medium
Ecru
Antique Blue light
Grey Green very light
Beaver Grey very light
Steel Grey light

Brown Grey very light
Beige Brown very light
Antique Blue very light
Shell Grey medium
Antique Blue ultra very light
Brown Grey light
Salmon very light
Antique Violet medium
Antique Mauve medium
Sportsman Flesh light

Stitch count: 191 X 153

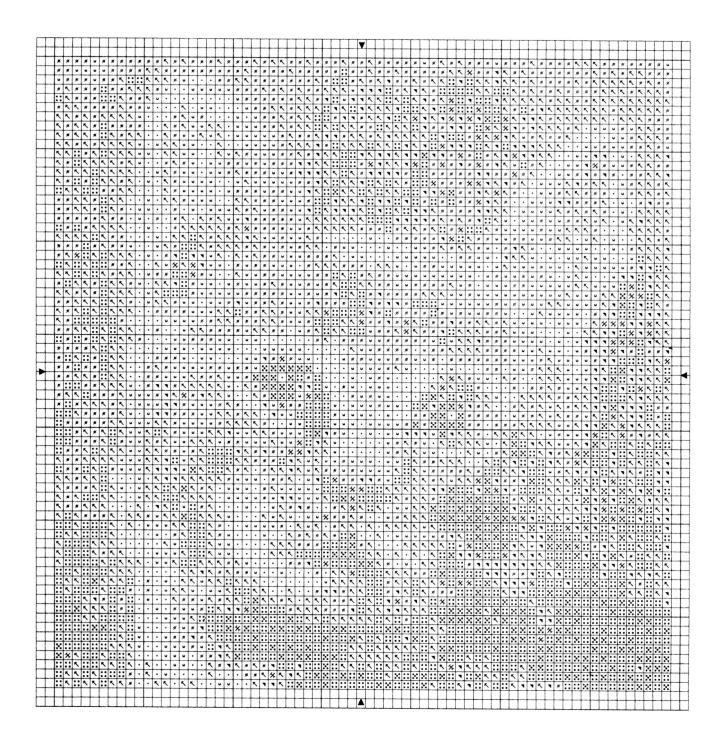

KEY

for herb pillow

↖ Antique Blue very light
⚹ Antique Violet very light
∷ Antique Blue light
ω Mocha Brown light
· Cream
◥ Beige Grey medium
∷ Steel Grey light
✕ Shell Grey medium

Stitch count: 69 x 68

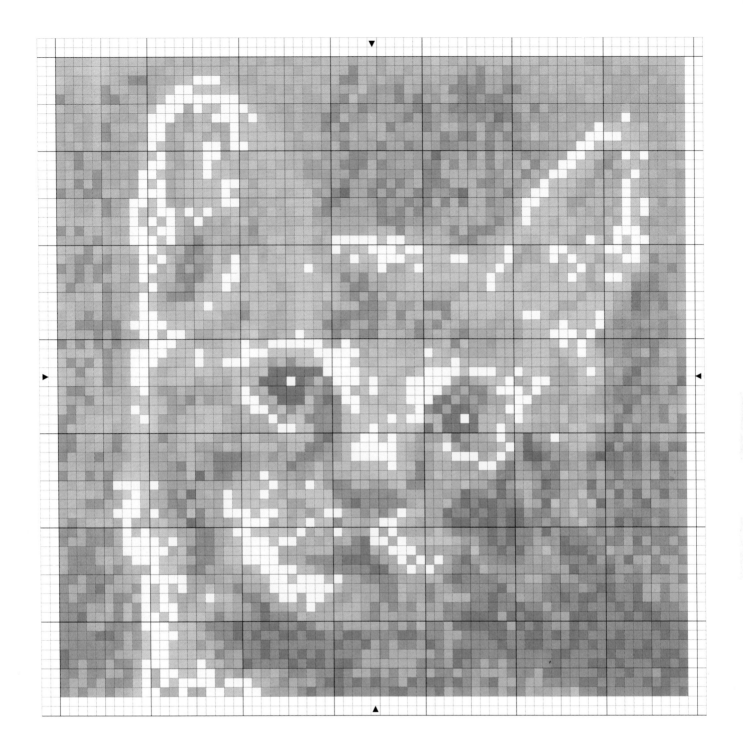

KEY

for herb pillow

- Antique Blue very light
- Antique Violet very light
- Antique Blue light
- Mocha Brown light
- Cream
- Beige Grey medium
- Steel Grey light
- Shell Grey medium

Stitch count: 69 x 68

KEY

for main project

- ↄ White
- ⌀ Antique Violet very light
- ⌃ Pearl Grey
- ⌄ Mocha Brown light
- S Antique Violet light
- ⌄ Pearl Grey very light
- · Off White
- ◣ Beige Grey medium
- ! Ecru
- ⋮⋮ Antique Blue light
- − Grey Green very light
- ⠠⠂ Beaver Grey very light
- ⣿ Steel Grey light
- ⁄ Brown Grey very light
- + Beige Brown very light
- ⤡ Antique Blue very light
- -⋅- Shell Grey medium
- ⠠⠄ Antique Blue ultra very light
- ✦ Brown Grey light
- ■ Salmon very light
- ⬤ Antique Violet medium
- ⋀ Antique Mauve medium
- ♡ Sportsman Flesh light

Stitch count: 191 X 153

CHAPTER 12
JENKS, THE MAINE COON ***

Size: 32 x 36 cm (13 x 14 in)
Embroidered by Marion Roden

Cats are distant, discreet, impeccably clean and are
able to stay silent. What more could be needed
to be in good company?
Marie Leczinska (Eighteenth Century)

The Maine Coon is one of the oldest breeds in America and originated in the state of Maine. It is one of the largest cats of all cat breeds, is very hardy and has a shaggy, long-haired coat. American folklore claims that this cat derives from the mating between the wild cat and the racoon, which explains the name 'Maine Coon.' This particular cat is called Jenks because the first recorded cat of this kind, in 1861 was called 'Captain Jenks'.

DESIGN CONSIDERATIONS

The content of a work of art finds its expression in the composition.

Wassily Kandinsky (1896–1944)

The word 'content' means the intention or inner meaning of the composition. Jenks needs to be expressed as powerful and hardy. Therefore, all three pairs of complementary colours are employed to produce this effect. In order to neutralise extremes of contrast, some of these colours are dull, compared with others which are bright. Furthermore, neutral browns and greys are interspersed throughout. Both devices also contribute to the overall harmony and unity of the composition.

MATERIALS

Aida, 14 count, 52 x 56 cm (20 x 22 in)
Tapestry needle, size 24
Roller (or 'tapestry') frame, wider than the fabric width
Strong sewing thread

METHOD

1. Prepare the aida, dress the frame (see pages 14–16) and mark the border and central lines.

2. Embroider in full cross stitch.

3. Once completed, lace, mount and frame the embroidery (see pages 18–19).

Threads									
Sranded Cottons	DMC	Anchor	Madeira	Skeins	Sranded Cottons	DMC	Anchor	Madeira	Skeins
Antique Gold light	3822	295	0109	5	Grey Green very light	928	274	1708	1
Yellow light	744	301	0112	2	Lemon light	445	288	0103	1
Dusty Rose	3354	74	0606	1	Hunter Green very light	3348	264	1409	1
Yellow Green light	733	280	1611	1	Terracotta dark	355	1014	2502	1
Tan medium light	437	362	2012	1	Coral light	351	10	0406	1
Beige Brown medium	840	379	2601	1	Topaz very light	727	293	0110	1
Old Gold light	676	891	2208	1	Violet dark	552	99	2714	1
White bright	B5200	1	2401	1	Mahogany very light	402	1047	2307	1
Coral very light	352	9	0303	1	Beaver Grey very dark	645	273	1811	1
Khaki Green light	3013	842	1605	1	Avocado Green pale	472	253	1604	1
Dusty Rose medium light	3733	75	0505	1	Misty Green light	3817	875	1702	1
Flesh very dark	3772	1007	2312	1	Yellow Green very light	734	279	1610	1
Golden Brown very light	3827	363	2301	1	Delft	809	130	0907	1
Peach light	3824	9575	0403	1	Khaki Green light	3013	842	1605	1

JENKS' HEAD (PEN HOLDER) **

The ideal of calm exists in a sitting cat.

Jules Renard (1864–1910)

DESIGN CONSIDERATIONS

Art in which precisely the lie is sanctified and the will to deception has a good conscience.

Friedrich Nietzsche (1844–1900)

Jenks has a calm aspect to his character as well as being powerfully hardy; such is the paradox of cats! In order to portray this aspect, a tranquil progression of cool grey tones is employed. However, these tones are lifted by a selection of warm violet colours. Why not try another colour scheme yourself which expresses your own feelings about Jenks' character? Remember, however, to match the tones when you change the hues, because you may lose the naturalistic effect.

MATERIALS

Aida, 16 count, 13 x 13 cm (5 x 5 in)

Tapestry needle, size 26

Embroidery hoop or rectangular stretcher frame
  11 x 11 cm (4½ x 4½ in)

Strong sewing thread

Pen holder (available from needlecraft suppliers)

Size: Diameter = 7.5 cm (3 in)
Embroidered by Jill Milne

Threads									
Sranded Cottons	DMC	Anchor	Madeira	Skeins	Sranded Cottons	DMC	Anchor	Madeira	Skeins
Beige Grey light	822	390	1908	1	Antique Blue light	932	1033	1710	1
Pearl Grey very light	762	234	1804	1	Antique Violet very light	3743	869	2611	1
Grey Green very light	928	274	1709	1	Steel Grey light	318	399	1802	1
Pearl Grey	415	398	1802	1	Beaver Grey light	648	900	1814	1
White	Blanc	2	2402	1	Grey Green medium	926	850	1707	1
Beaver Grey very light	3072	847	1805	1	Sea Foam Green medium	502	876	1703	1
Grey Green light	927	848	1708	1	Pewter Grey	317	400	1714	1
Sea Foam Green					Beaver Grey medium	647	1040	1813	1
medium light	3813	875	1701	1	Beaver Grey dark	646	8581	1812	1

JENKS, THE MAINE COON

METHOD

1. Prepare the aida and the embroidery hoop or stretcher frame (see pages 14-16). Mark out the border and central lines.

2. Embroider in full cross stitch.

3. When you have finished the embroidery, remove it from the frame and press it if necessary. Trim the excess fabric leaving a 1 cm (½ in) margin around the edge of the design. Instructions for placing the embroidery in the pen holder will be provided by the supplier. The one illustrated here is from Framecraft (see List of Suppliers, page 143).

KEY

for pen holder

- Beige Grey light
- Pearl Grey very light
- Grey Green very light
- Pearl Grey
- White
- Beaver Grey very light
- Grey Green light
- Sea Foam Green medium light
- Antique Blue light
- Antique Violet very light
- Steel Grey light
- Beaver Grey light
- Grey Green medium
- Sea Foam Green medium
- Pewter Grey
- Beaver Grey medium
- Beaver Grey dark

Stitch count: 51 x 51

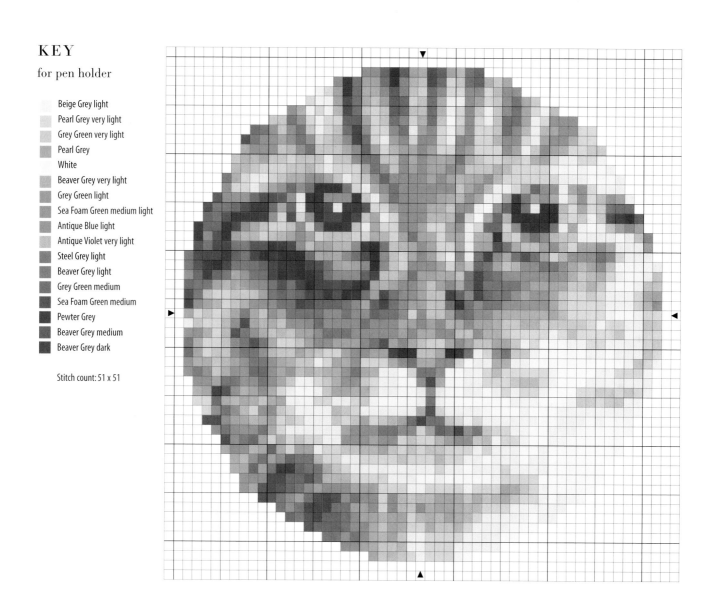

KEY

for pen holder

! Beige Grey light
∧ Pearl Grey very light
— Grey Green very light
▲ Pearl Grey
• White
✓ Beaver Grey very light
✗ Grey Green light
↑ Sea Foam Green medium light
⠒ Antique Blue light
∅ Antique Violet very light
⠢ Steel Grey light
||| Beaver Grey light
☐ Grey Green medium
▼ Sea Foam Green medium
◼ Pewter Grey
✕ Beaver Grey medium
◑ Beaver Grey dark

Stitch count: 51 x 51

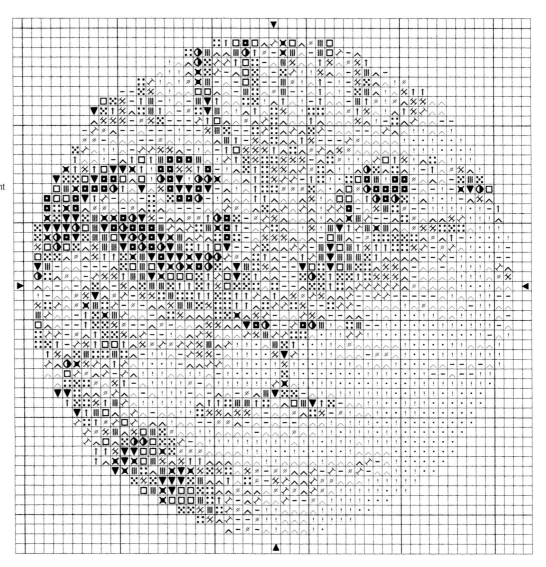

Though we work for days or years

Neither the other hinders;

Each is competent and hence

Enjoys his skill in silence.

from *The Scholar and his Cat*, Anonymous (circa AD 750),

translated from the Irish by Frank O'Connor

KEY
for main project

Antique Gold light
Yellow light
Dusty Rose
Yellow Green light
Tan medium light
Beige Brown medium
Old Gold light
White bright
Coral very light
Khaki Green light
Dusty Rose medium light
Flesh very dark
Golden Brown very light
Peach light
Jade
Lemon light
Hunter Green very light
Terracotta dark
Coral light
Topaz very light
Violet dark
Mahogany very light
Beaver Grey very dark
Avocado Green pale
Misty Green light
Yellow Green very light
Delft
Khaki Green light

Stitch count: 156 X 202

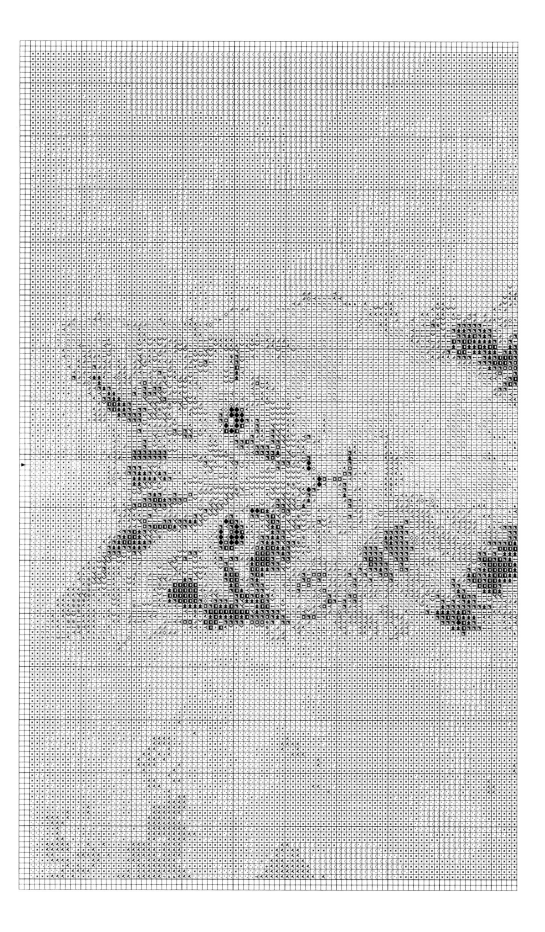

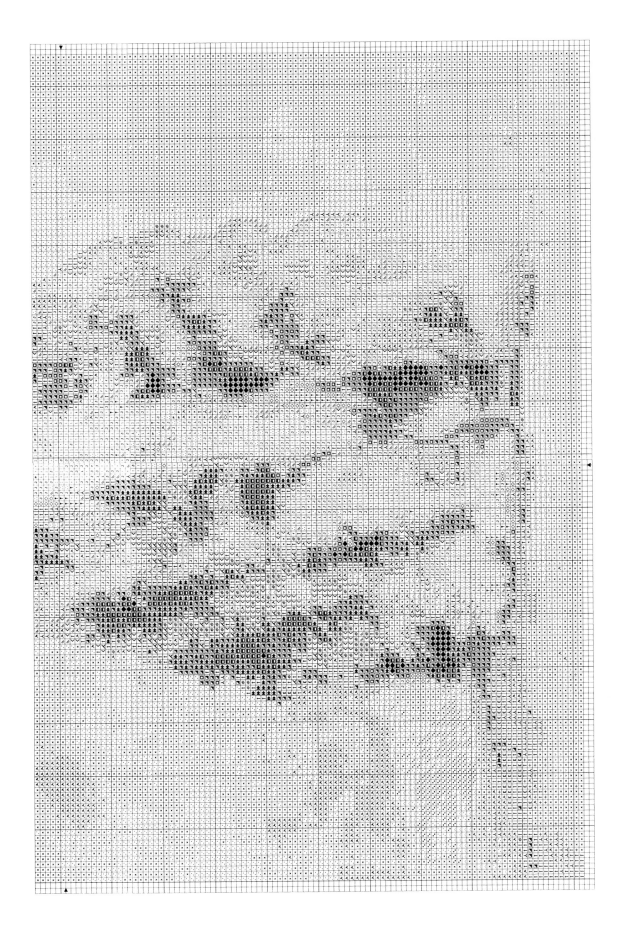

CHAPTER 13
TOM, THE TABBY-AND-WHITE CAT ***

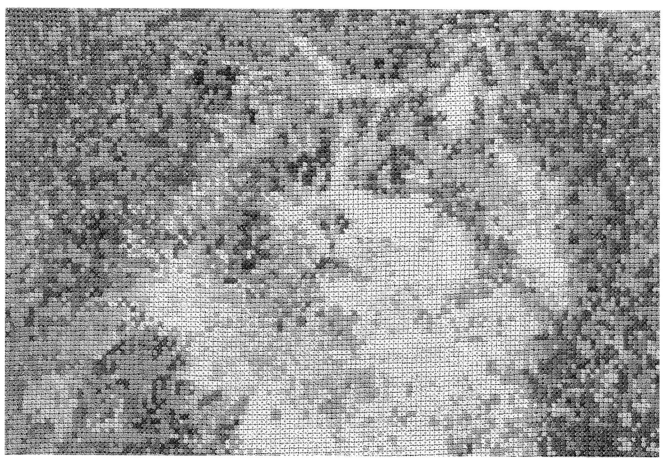

Size: 26 x 21 cm (10¼ x 8¼ in)
Embroidered by Sue Fielding
(detail only shown)

Stately, kindly, lordly friend,

Condescend

Here to sit by me, and turn

Golden eyes, love's lustrous mead,

On the golden page I read.

From *To a Cat* by Algernon Charles Swinburn (1837–1909)

TOM, THE TABBY-AND-WHITE CAT

Beatrix Potter's book *Tom Kitten* has inspired many cat owners to call their male cat 'Tom' or 'Tommy'. 'Tom cat' as a general term given to a male cat has an earlier ancestry; the origin can be traced back to exactly 1760 when an anonymous story called *The Life and Adventures of a Cat* was published. The male feline hero, then known as the 'ram cat' was called 'Tom the Cat'. Because the story was so popular everyone started to replace the original word 'ram' with 'Tom' and this continues today. Like all long-haired cats Tom has a lustrous coat with a ruff about his neck. He has eyes which, I am sure you have noticed, are 'golden'.

DESIGN CONSIDERATIONS

*That each part of a work of art has its own particular
arrangement it is not enough;
they must all agree together and make but one
harmonious whole.*
From *The Principles of Painting* (1743) by Roger de Piles

The composition is intended to express an immediate impact of a typically proud, self-assured Tom Cat. At the same time, Tom is to appear graceful, elegant and appealing. Therefore, many contrasting hues, tones and intensities of colour are included. However, they are also repeated in various groupings, progressions and proportions throughout the composition. It is the balance between contrast and repetition of these three aspects of colour which realise all aspects of Tom's character and which also need to 'agree together' and make 'but one harmonious whole.'

This project is one of the more complex ones, but do not let this deter you from attempting to embroider it. Allow yourself several months to execute it. Should any negative thoughts enter your mind, such as 'this is far too difficult', replace it with positive thoughts such as that from Albert Einstein who said 'In the middle of difficulties lies opportunity'. You will then be making a huge step in your creative development.

MATERIALS

Aida, 14 count, 40 x 35 cm (15¾ x 13¾ in)

Tapestry needle, size 24

Roller (or 'tapestry') frame, wider than the fabric width

Strong sewing thread

Threads										
Sranded Cottons	**DMC**	**Anchor**	**Madeira**	**Skeins**		**Sranded Cottons**	**DMC**	**Anchor**	**Madeira**	**Skeins**
Mocha Brown medium dark	3032	903	2002	2		Avocado Green pale	472	(253)	1414	1
Delft dark	798	131	0911	2		Avocado Green very light	471	266	1501	1
Beige Grey medium	644	830	1814	2		Antique Mauve very light	778	968	0808	1
Drab Brown medium	612	832	2108	2		Flesh dark	3064	883	1603	2
Sky Blue very light	747	158	1104	1		Beige Brown dark	839	(360)	1913	1
Green Grey light	3053	858	1510	1		Jade light	563	208	1207	1
Beaver Grey very dark	645	273	1811	1		Antique Mauve medium	316	1017	0809	2
Fern Green very light	524	858	1511	2		Old Gold light	676	891	2208	1
White bright	B5200	1	2401	2		Blue Violet light	341	117	0901	1
Wedgwood medium	518	1039	1106	2		Avocado light	372	853	2110	1
Khaki Green medium	3012	844	1606	1		Golden Brown very light	3827	363	2301	1
Beige Brown very light	842	376	1910	2		Violet medium	553	98	0712	1
Pistachio Green very light	369	1043	1309	1		Flesh very dark	3772	1007	2312	1
Yellow ultra very light	3823	386	2511	1		Mauve very light	3609	85	0710	1
Beige Brown medium	840	379	1912	1		Sage Green light	3819	278	1414	1
Antique Mauve dark	315	1017	0810	1		Copper light	921	(884)	2305	1

METHOD

1. Prepare the aida, dress the frame (see pages 14–16) and mark the border and central lines.

2. Embroider in full cross stitch.

3. Once completed, frame, mount and lace the embroidery (see pages 18–19).

Note: Because of the complexity of this design you will find it beneficial to start embroidering from the lower edge and work towards the upper edge. Furthermore, begin with the darker colours first which will give you clear reference points for subsequent counting.

TOM'S FACE (PAPERWEIGHT) **

Size: 5 x 5 cm (2 x 2 in)
Embroidered by Pat Ripley

The cat is the only animal without visible means of support
who still manages to find a living in the city.

Carl Van Vechten (1880–1914)

DESIGN CONSIDERATIONS

In quietness and in confidence shall be your strength.
Isaiah 30 : 15

If you look at the number of colours used to represent
Tom's quiet and confident strength in this little project, you
will see they are considerably reduced compared with the
main project. Consequently, you will find it moderately
simple to embroider, especially if you continue to work in a
quiet atmosphere, which is conducive to the development of
your confidence and strength in your creative skills.

MATERIALS

Aida, 20 count, 15 x 15 cm (6 x 6 in)

Tapestry needle, size 26

Embroidery hoop, 12 cm (5 in) in diameter

Paperweight (available from needlework suppliers)

Threads				
Sranded Cottons	**DMC**	**Anchor**	**Madeira**	**Skeins**
Yellow ultra very light	3823	386	2512	1
Khaki Green medium	3012	844	1617	1
Fern Green very light	524	858	1512	1
Beige Brown very light	842	376	1910	1
Beaver Grey very dark	645	273	1811	1
Beige Grey medium	644	830	2001	1
Beige Brown medium	840	379	2601	1
Avocado Green pale	472	(253)	1414	1
Sky Blue very light	747	158	1104	1

METHOD

1. Prepare the aida, the embroidery hoops (see pages 14–15) and mark out the borders and central lines.

2. Embroider in full cross stitch.

3. When you have finished the embroidery, remove it from the embroidery hoop and press it if necessary. Instructions for attaching the embroidery to the paper weight will be provided by the supplier. The one illustrated here is from Framecraft (see List of Suppliers, page 143).

He is a full lecherous beast in youth, swift, pliant and merry …and is led by a straw and playeth therewith: and is a right heary beast in age and fully sleepy, and lyeth slyly in wait of mice…In time of love he is hard fighting for wives, and one rendeth the other grievously with biting and with claws. And he maketh a rueful noise and ghastful when one proffereth to fight another…

Bartholomaeus Anglicus, *De Propietatibus Rerum* (circa 1230)

KEY

for main project

■	Mocha Brown medium dark
	White bright
■	Delft dark
■	Drab Brown medium
■	Beige Grey medium
	Sky Blue very light
■	Green Grey light
■	Beaver Grey very dark
■	Fern Green very light
■	Wedgwood medium
■	Khaki Green medium
■	Beige Brown very light

	Pistachio Green very light
	Yellow ultra very light
■	Beige Brown medium
■	Antique Mauve dark
■	Avocado Green pale
■	Avocado Green very light
■	Antique Mauve very light
■	Flesh dark
■	Beige Brown dark
■	Jade light
■	Antique Mauve medium
■	Old Gold light

■	Blue Violet light
■	Avocado light
■	Golden Brown very light
■	Violet medium
■	Flesh very dark
■	Mauve very light
■	Sage Green light
■	Copper light

Stitch count: 143 x 116

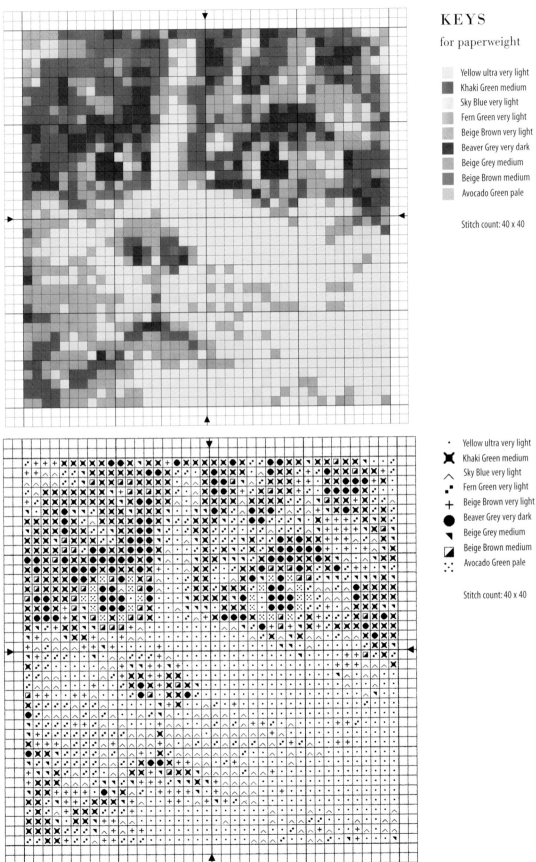

KEYS

for paperweight

- Yellow ultra very light
- Khaki Green medium
- Sky Blue very light
- Fern Green very light
- Beige Brown very light
- Beaver Grey very dark
- Beige Grey medium
- Beige Brown medium
- Avocado Green pale

Stitch count: 40 x 40

- · Yellow ultra very light
- ✖ Khaki Green medium
- ⌃ Sky Blue very light
- ▪· Fern Green very light
- + Beige Brown very light
- ● Beaver Grey very dark
- ◣ Beige Grey medium
- ◪ Beige Brown medium
- ∴ Avocado Green pale

Stitch count: 40 x 40

KEY

for main project

- Σ   Mocha Brown medium dark
- ✕   White bright
- ◑   Delft dark
- <   Drab Brown medium
- ◣   Beige Grey medium
- ∧   Sky Blue very light
- ⣏   Green Grey light
- ●   Beaver Grey very dark
- ■   Fern Green very light
- ▼   Wedgwood medium
- ✕   Khaki Green medium
- +   Beige Brown very light
- ˙'   Pistachio Green very light
- ▪   Yellow ultra very light
- ◪   Beige Brown medium
- ▣   Antique Mauve dark
- ᴘ   Avocado Green pale
- ∩   Avocado Green very light
- ⟍   Antique Mauve very light
- N   Flesh dark
- ▥   Beige Brown dark
- ∧   Jade light
- ‖‖   Antique Mauve medium
- ♡   Old Gold light
- ɢ   Blue Violet light
- ○   Avocado light
- ⩗   Golden Brown very light
- ⊥   Violet medium
- ⫻   Flesh very dark
- ᵣ   Mauve very light
- ᵃ   Sage Green light
- ✦   Copper light

Stitch count: 143 X 116

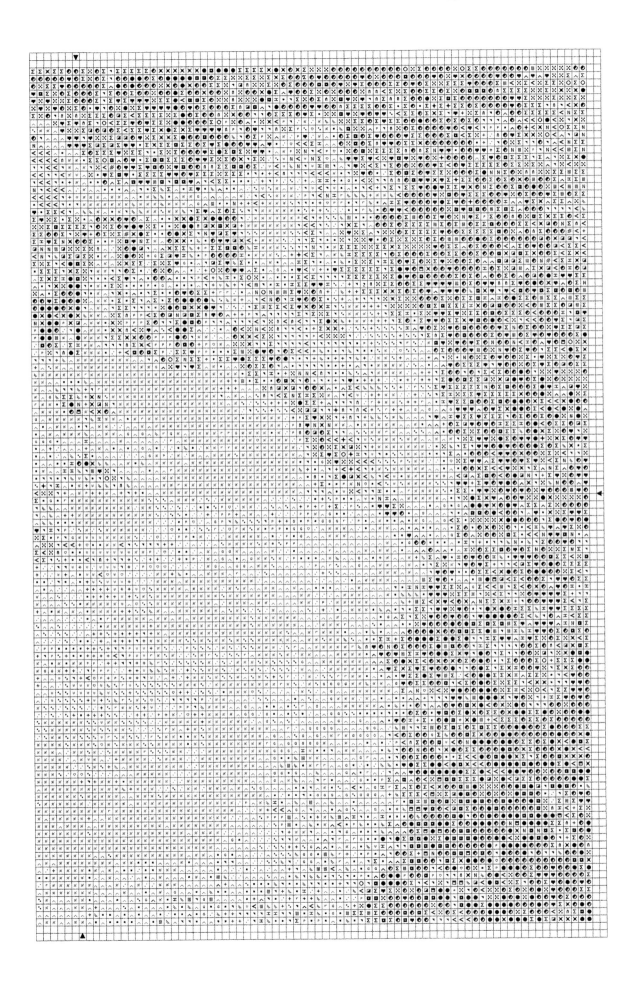

141

BIBLIOGRAPHY

Alford, Lady Marion, M, *Needlework as Art*, Samson Low 1886, republished by E.P. Publishing Ltd 1975

Beazley, Angela, *Next Steps in Cross Stitch*, Merehurst Limited 1996

Benham, Gurney, W, *Cassell's Classified Quotations*, Cassell 1921

Bloomfield, Janet, *The Concise Dictionary of Cats*, Linkline 1977

Byrne, Robert and Skelton, Teresa, *Quotable Cats*, Hamlyn 1985

Christie, Mrs Archibald, *Embroidery and Tapestry Weaving*, John Hogg 1906

Christie, Mrs Archibald, *Samplers and Stitches*, B.T. Batsford 1920

Clutton-Brock, Juliet, *The British Museum Book of Cats*, British Museum Publications Ltd 1988

Cutts, Paddy, *Cats*, Sunburst Books 1993

Day, Lewis, F, *Art in Needlework*, B.T. Batsford 1900

Foster, Dorothy, *In Praise of Cats*, Harrap 1975

Hasler, Julie, *Julie Hasler's Cross Stitch Projects*, B.T. Batsford 1996

Jones, Owen, *The Grammar of Ornament*, Day and Son 1856, republished by Omega Books Ltd 1986

Loxton, Howard, *Beautiful Cats*, Sundial Books Ltd 1979

Morris, Desmond, *Cat Watching*, Ebury Press 1994

Moore, Joan, *The Cats Lovers Companion*, Colour Library Books Ltd 1993

Murray, Peter and Linda, *A Dictionary of Art and Artists*, Penguin 1975

Nichols, Beverley, (foreword) *All About Cats*, Orbis 1974

Pollard, Anna, *Cats*, Treasure Press 1990

Raleigh, Ivor, et al, *Practical Guide to Cats*, Hamlyn 1976

Sayer, Angela, *The World of Cats*, Optimum Books 1982

Wratten, Peggy, *Cats*, International Ltd 1977

Wood, James, *The Nuttall Dictionary of Quotations*, Frederick Warne 1930

Verso, Jo, *Jo Verso's Complete Cross Stitch Course*, David and Charles 1996

LIST OF SUPPLIERS

Artisan
Battlers Green Farm Road
Common Lane
Radlett
Hertfordshire WD7 8PH
Tel: 01923 853327

Barnyards Ltd
PO Box 28
Thirsk
North Yorkshire YO7 3YN
Tel: 01845 524344

Choices
36 Meadowside Road
Pangbourne
Reading
Berkshire RG8 7NH
Tel: 01734 843122

Coats Craft UK
PO Box 22
The Lingfield Estate
McMullen Road
Darlington
Co. Durham DL1 1YQ
Tel: 01325 365457

DMC Creative World Ltd
Pullman Road
Wigston
Leicestershire LE18 2DY
Tel: 01162 811040

Framecraft
372–376 Summer Lane
Hockley
Birmingham B19 3QA
Tel: 01212 120551

Francesca Lawrence
Cae Gwydd
Meolfre
Clwyd LL22 9DU
Tel: 01745 824358

Madeira Threads UK
PO Box 6
Thirsk
North Yorkshire YO7 3YN
Tel: 01845 524880

The Needlecraft Centre
Longleat
Warminster
Wiltshire BA12 7NL
Tel: 01985 844774

Simply Scissors
24 Walker Close
New Southgate
London N11 1AQ
Tel: 0181 368 5596

Speciality Needlecraft
58a Albert Street
Biddulph
Staffordshire ST8 6DU
Tel: 01782 519936

*West End Lace and
Embroidery Supplies*
Orchid Cottage
Drury Lane
Mortimer Common
Reading
Berkshire RG7 2JN
Tel: 01189 332670

Voirrey Embroidery
Brinstage Hall
Wirral
Cheshire L63 6JA
Tel: 01513 423514

INDEX